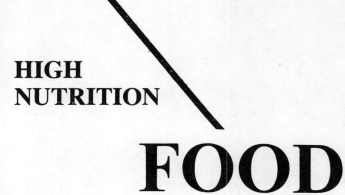

HIGH NUTRITION

FOOD

LOW COST

Solomon Garb M.D.

Scientific Director
American Medical Center at Denver

SPRINGER PUBLISHING COMPANY · **New York**

Springer Publishing Company, Inc.
200 Park Avenue South
New York, N.Y. 10003

75 76 77 78 79 / 10 9 8 7 6 5 4 3 2 1

Library of Congress Cataloging in Publication Data

Garb, Solomon.
  Food: high nutrition, low cost.

  1. Food. 2. Nutrition. 3. Cookery. I. Title.
TX353.G3   641.3   74-26514
ISBN 0-8261-1750-3

Printed in the United States of America

CONTENTS

ACKNOWLEDGMENTS

I am grateful to Ms. Carson Justice for research assistance, to Ms. Martha Morris for typing, to Mses. Barbara Hansen, Carson Justice, and Sandra Clift for testing and adjusting recipes, and to Gordon Garb for computer programming and consultations.

INTRODUCTION

When the average weekly cost of food for a family rises by $10, most people realize that they are paying too much. This book is addressed to those who wish to cut down on their food bills without sacrificing high nutritional values in the process. It is not intended as a specialized diet book or a gourmet cookbook. In order to know which foods are more desirable nutritionally than others, some knowledge of the basic components of food is necessary, and a chapter is devoted to this topic. Other chapters are intended to serve as guides for shopping and preparing food, and several food-value charts plus a section of recipes are included.

By following the suggestions in this book, a family could save as much as 25% to 30% of their annual food bill. The savings accrued would benefit not only the individual householder, but every penny saved would also help to retard the vicious cycle of rising prices and help the country.

The rapid rise in food prices is one of the most obvious aspects of inflation, as it has affected all Americans directly and substantially. The origins of this alarming cost increase are largely to be found in current governmental policies, alternatives to which are discussed in a chapter at the end of this book.

Until a comprehensive revision of this country's agricultural program is developed and implemented, the wise use of this book should help families make substantial savings in their food budgets.

Chapter 1

FOODS AND NUTRITION

There are several basic components of foods. The major nutrients on a weight basis are carbohydrates, fats, and proteins. Other components include vitamins and minerals. Although these are present in relatively small concentrations, they are nevertheless essential to normal growth and health.

CARBOHYDRATES

Sugars and starches are the important carbohydrates in human nutrition. Starches are digested to sugars before they can be absorbed into the blood, so that their effect on body metabolism is essentially that of sugars. Sugars provide energy in the form of calories for muscular activity, nerve conduction, and other aspects of cellular function. Each gram of carbohydrate produces 4.1 calories. The body can store only a limited amount of carbohydrate. Any carbohydrate that is not used for energy, or that cannot be stored, is changed into fat and stored as such. It takes slightly over two grams of carbohydrate to produce one gram of fat.

In the absence of adequate carbohydrate in the diet, fat can be changed to carbohydrate. However, this is a somewhat slow process. If the diet has excess protein, it is changed to carbohydrate. However, the human body *cannot change carbohydrates back to protein*. Only plants and some bacteria can do this.

Carbohydrates should form the major part of the food intake of most people. Exceptions are persons living in extremely cold climates, such as Eskimos, and those who require a food intake equal to 5,000 calories per day or more, such as lumberjacks. The major component of their diet has to be fat.

There are many misconceptions about carbohydrates which must be avoided if a healthy diet that is also economical is to be followed. A common misleading belief is that starchy foods are particularly fattening, when, in fact, *all* foods can be fattening if eaten to excess. Starches have the identical caloric value as sugars and proteins, 4.1 calories per gram. Therefore, *starches are no more fattening than sugars or protein*. Fats have a much higher caloric value—9.3 calories per gram. Therefore, starches are less than half as fattening as fats.

Another misconception is that the so-called "starchy" foods are purely starch, when actually some of them contain important amounts of protein. For example, a pound of dry spaghetti or noodles as purchased contains 57 grams of protein, while a pound of bacon contains only 38 grams of protein.* Since spaghetti and noodles are much less expensive than bacon, it follows that they are much better buys. Even the best cuts of choice beef have only about 58 to 90 grams of protein per pound, depending on how meticulously the fat is removed. By contrast, a pound of ordinary dried navy beans contains 101 grams of protein. It is quite true that the beans are *mainly* starch, containing 278 grams of starch per pound, but their protein content is higher than that of beef, pork, lamb, or poultry. Since dried beans are much cheaper than these meats, they are definitely much better buys. Despite the water added to canned beans, they are usually better buys for protein content than meats.

One other major way to save money on food is to eat more bread, appropriately called the "staff of life." Although mainly starch, bread contains about 40 grams of protein per pound—more than bacon, and about half as much per pound as

---

*It should be noted that all comparisons are based on a *pound* of food *as purchased*, because this is appropriate to a consideration of relative costs.

most meats. Since a pound of bread is still relatively inexpensive, it is clearly more economical than meat.

FATS

Fats also provide energy, but in a more limited fashion. Nerve cells, including those in the brain, cannot use fats for energy. They must have sugar (glucose) exclusively. Fats are also needed for other aspects of body function, but only in relatively small amounts, and this need not be considered in terms of the costs of food.

Recent evidence suggests that there are important differences between saturated and unsaturated fats. The term "saturated" refers to the degree to which the carbon atoms in the fatty acids are attached to hydrogen, but for practical nutritional purposes, it is enough to know whether a fat is largely saturated or unsaturated. In general, *saturated fats tend to be solid at refrigerator temperatures*. Beef fat, pork fat, butter, and cheese fat are examples. One important saturated fat, coconut oil, is liquid at refrigerator temperatures.

The available evidence from many sources involving animal and human studies points overwhelmingly to a direct relationship between the intake of saturated fats and the occurrence of arterial disease and heart attacks. This relationship is based on cholesterol deposition in the arteries. There may be other causes of heart attacks, but the eating of saturated fats seems to be the main one. *Therefore, it is prudent to keep the intake of saturated fat as low as possible.*

Unsaturated fats are generally liquid at refrigerator temperatures. They include corn, soybean, cottonseed, safflower, olive, and peanut oil, fish oils, and the oils in most nuts and vegetables (except coconuts). Hydrogenation changes an unsaturated fat to a saturated fat, so that hydrogenated vegetable oils are the equivalent of saturated fats. Some margarines contain a mixture of hydrogenated and unhydrogenated vegetable oils for the sake of consistency. They are preferable to butter—which is highly saturated—but not as good as the liquid oils. Therefore, one could use these margarines as a spread on bread, but for cooking it would be preferable to use the unsaturated vegetable oils.

Since each gram of fat provides 9.3 calories, more than *twice* as many as a gram of carbohydrate or protein, fats are the most fattening foods. People who should not gain weight should restrict their fat intake.

In some foods, other substances are found in conjunction with fats, some of which are helpful, and others of which are not. Examples of helpful substances are the fat-soluble vitamins, such as vitamins A and D. A harmful substance found in conjunction with fats is cholesterol, which forms deposits inside the lining of the arteries. The two foods which contain enough cholesterol to warrant special caution in the amount consumed are brains and egg yolk.

PROTEINS

Proteins are much more complex molecules than carbohydrates or fats. They are the building and rebuilding blocks of the body cells. Proteins are also needed to produce the enzymes that carry out body functions, both inside and outside of cells. Only small amounts of protein can be stored in the body, so that protein deprivation for more than a few days leads to body wasting, as some body cells are used to keep others functioning. Excess protein in the diet is converted to carbohydrate and used for energy. However, animals are not able to make proteins from other foods. Each gram of protein has a caloric value of 4.1 calories when used for energy, just like a gram of carbohydrate.

Proteins are composed of combinations of amino acids, and there are 21 different amino acids that make up mammalian proteins. Of these, some are immediately essential to growth and life, while others are not, since they are obtained from the breakdown of the more complex ones. Most animal foods contain these amino acids in a good proportion for efficient use by the body. They are called proteins of high biological value. Some vegetable proteins have the amino acids present in a proportion that is less efficient, and consequently have a lower biological value. However, proteins of low and high biological value in combination can complement each other. For this and other reasons, it is usually advisable to have a mixture of proteins in a meal. For example, corn's protein alone has a low biological value, but, when corn is eaten with beans, the beans supply the extra amino acids, so that the mixture has a high biological value. I suspect that our instinctive, inherited tastes recognize this, since succotash, a mixture of corn and lima beans, is quite popular.

It isn't necessary to become too analytical about the amino acids of various proteins, since the protein allowance in the American diet is quite high. The proteins of low biological value are usable, and as there are some proteins in almost all foods, these can help fill in any deficiencies. A basic rule should be that if beans or peas are eaten at a meal, some corn or other grain such as bread should also be eaten at the same meal. If this simple rule is followed, one will in all likelihood take in enough protein of the right type for good health.

A common misconception about protein-containing foods concerns the concentration of protein. We are accustomed to foods that have a high concentration of carbohydrates or fat. Some concentrated carbohydrate foods can be more than 95% carbohydrate, and some concentrated fatty foods can be more than 95% fat. However, when we refer to high protein foods, we are dealing with much lower concentrations. Lean meats seldom contain more than 25% protein as purchased, or more than 33% after the fat has been cooked out. Parmesan cheese, the highest in protein, has 36% protein. Dried, nonfat milk also contains 36% protein. These are about the highest protein concentrations to be found in ordinary foods available in stores. Protein also happens to be a more expensive nutrient than carbohydrates or fat.

VITAMINS

Vitamins are essential nutrients that are needed in relatively low amounts. The usual daily adult requirement is an estimate that changes periodically, and in regard to some vitamins, has not been established. In any event, it is generally recognized that one can take less than half or more than twice the recommended vitamin intake and remain in excellent health.

In general, nutrition experts agree that vitamins should come from natural foods whenever possible. On the other hand, I can see no important objection to taking a standard dose of vitamin pills as a dietary supplement, especially if it makes a person feel psychologically better. The money spent on vitamin pills may be wasted, but it is a comparatively small expenditure.

MINERALS

Minerals are essential nutrients present in most foods, and often in water. With a reasonably varied diet, one ought not develop any mineral deficiency. Deficiencies in iron and calcium do occur at times, but they are not related to the cost of food, since some inexpensive foods are quite high in iron and calcium content.

CALORIE

A calorie is a measure of the energy provided by the metabolism of food. Strictly speaking, a calorie is the amount of energy needed to raise the temperature of one gram of water by one degree Centigrade. This unit is too small for practical purposes, however, and a kilocalorie—one thousand times as great—is commonly used. Gradually, the prefix "kilo" was omitted, and now when the energy value of foods is discussed, *calorie means the amount of energy needed to raise 1,000 grams of water (a kilogram) one degree Centigrade.* In this book, we will follow the common usage. To give the reader some idea of the amount of energy involved in ordinary terms, to raise the temperature of a quart of water from just above freezing to just under boiling temperature, requires approximately 100 calories.

"Empty Calories"

The phrase "empty calories" was coined by certain people to denote a food that provides calories, but little or no protein or vitamins. It is basically an emotional, misleading term that confuses the issue. There is no such thing as an "empty calorie." A calorie is a term having precise, scientific meaning. It is a measure of the heat energy supplied by a foodstuff. It is not a measure of volume, and therefore cannot be either empty or full. This phrase should be ignored.

"Nutritious But Low in Calories"

This is another misconception widely promoted by advertisers. The caloric value of a food is one measure of its nutritional content. A food high in protein *cannot* be low in calories, since protein has 4.1 calories per gram, exactly the same caloric value as sugar. This phrase then is roughly equivalent to saying that something is heavy, but low in pounds. Slogans of this sort are dreamed up by advertising agencies to induce people to buy expensive foods.

REFINED FOODS

It is currently fashionable to complain that the American diet has too many refined foods, but the fact is that the main bulk of the American diet is no more highly refined than it was hundreds of years ago. Only two major foods in this country are highly refined—sugar and some baked goods.* By its nature, sugar has to be refined. It would be quite impractical to put sugar cane or sugar beets into coffee, tea, or other items to be flavored.

Baked goods are generally made of refined white flour. It is quite true that chemical analyses of whole wheat show more vitamins than are found in white flour. These vitamins are largely in the outer layers which are discarded in the refining process. On the other hand, *it has not been proven that the vitamins in the outer layers of wheat are fully utilized by humans*. These outer layers are not completely digested, and many of the vitamins may be unavailable. The practice of adding vitamins to white flour provides substantial amounts of several important vitamins, and seems a reasonable procedure.

*Rice is sometimes included, but it is not a major item of diet for most Americans.

Regarding the remainder of the American diet, are apples, oranges, bananas, peaches, plums, melons, or other fruits refined in any factory? The green peas, beans, carrots, cabbage, squash, spinach, yams, potatoes, cucumbers, onions, and other vegetables eaten by Americans are no more refined than those eaten by their remote ancestors. The beef, pork, lamb, chicken, turkey, and fish have not had any vitamins or minerals removed. When the total American diet is considered, the charge of over-refining is clearly unsubstantiated.

ECONOMICAL FOODS ARE NOT NECESSARILY FATTENING

Many Americans are aware of the dangers of obesity, but unfortunately this concern is accompanied by a great deal of misinformation about overweight and its relation to certain foods.

It takes approximately 3,300 calories in excess of a balanced diet to produce a pound of fat. (Human fat is not pure; it contains some bound water.) A person will gain weight if more food is consumed than is used in energy and waste production, *regardless of the type of food eaten.*

The concentrated food energy of fat, however, is seldom fully recognized. A gram of pure protein, sugar, or starch provides 4.1 calories. A gram of pure fat, on the other hand, provides 9.3 calories, 227% as much. *Most Americans who are overweight became that way through eating excessive amounts of fat.* Indeed, the average American diet provides about 40% of its calories as fat, when a theoretically healthy ideal would be 20%.

Much of this fat is not readily identifiable. Lean hamburger, for instance, provides 219 calories per 100 grams after cooking. Of these, 103 calories come from fat. Forty-seven per cent of the total calories are fat-derived. In a salad served with one of the most common dressings, 80 to 87% of the calories come from fat. In a Danish pastry, the figure is 51%. Few people realize how many of the calories in some "sweets" actually come from fat rather than from sugar. In milk chocolate, for example, 57% of the calories come from fat. Finally, although nuts do provide a substantial source of protein, most of their food energy comes from fat—in dried almonds, 82%, and in pecans, 94%! Since all of these examples are of relatively expensive foods, there is no reason to believe that expensive foods are less fattening than economical foods.

Some of the constantly repeated statements about certain foods are highly misleading. "Potatoes are fattening" is one of them. In themselves, potatoes are *less* fattening than most foods eaten by Americans. Most of the calories in potatoes as served come not from the potatoes themselves, but from the butter added in mashing, or the oil or fat added in frying. Similarly, the oil or fat in the sauce added to spaghetti often contributes more calories than the spaghetti itself.

Another problem is that most people are not aware of the amount of water absorbed by certain foods in cooking. For many foods, such as vegetables, meat, poultry, and eggs, the weight after cooking is about the same as the weight before cooking. Therefore, the calories per 100 grams remain the same. However, with some dried foods, notably macaroni, spaghetti, rice, and dried beans, large amounts of water are absorbed. For example, cooked spaghetti absorbs more than twice its own weight in water. Therefore, a pound of cooked spaghetti has only 30% as many calories as a pound of spaghetti as purchased, and a pound of cooked navy beans has only about 35% as many calories as a pound of dried, uncooked beans. Unless these changes are understood, the assessment of weight gain potential in these foods can be greatly exaggerated.

Finally, there is the problem caused by constant repetition of misleading statements. When a person has heard for years that "potatoes are fattening," it is understandable that he or she may come to believe it.

In the table at the end of this chapter are listed some foods commonly referred to as "fattening," and some which usually escape that designation. The tabulation is based on the 3,300 calories needed in excess of a balanced diet to produce a pound of body fat.

It should be clear that there is no consistent relationship between the cost of various foods and their fattening propensities.

Table I Amount of certain foods an adult must eat in addition to a balanced diet to gain one pound of weight

Food	Number of pounds that must be eaten in addition to a balanced diet to gain one pound
American cheese, plain	2
Baked potatoes, plain	8
Boiled potatoes, plain	11
Bread, white, plain	2 ¾
Cooked navy beans, plain	6 ⅛
Cooked rice, plain	6 ⅔
Cooked spaghetti, plain	6 ½
Hamburger, lean, cooked	3 ½
Hamburger, regular, cooked	2 ½
Pecans	1
Porterhouse or T-bone steak, cooked	1 ⅞
Round roast, cooked	3 ⅞
Sirloin steak, cooked	1 ⅞
Swiss cheese, plain	2
Tuna fish in oil	2 ½

Chapter 2

PURCHASING AND STORING
FOOD WISELY

In this chapter we will consider some points relating to the way in which food should be purchased. In general, you should try to economize on every purchase, not just in one area. It makes little sense to save money on meat and then spend it on some fancy food item that in its own way is overpriced. It is also necessary to compare the nutritional values of the food you are buying. Although meat was priced at about 1 to 1½ times its true value in May, 1973, the cost of many other foods was 2 to 4 times their value based on nutritive content. Some specific comparisons are given in this chapter, and these relationships for many foods are expressed in the "Food-Value Counter" (p. 30).

WHO SHOULD BUY

If the woman of the house is handling the food budget, it may be most practical for her to do all the major shopping for the household. Some husbands may overbuy, or be tempted by gourmet items, and many children pressure their mothers into buying overpriced and undernourishing items such as potato chips, jelly rolls, sodas, and so forth.

It may be necessary to explain to children the misleading nature of certain television advertising about food, since the manufacturers are not currently fulfilling their public responsibility in that area.

11

Ideally, the whole family should be educated about nutritional values, and develop a cooperative attitude as to the family's nutritional and economic goals.

WHERE TO BUY FOODS

In general, it is most economical and convenient to buy foods in a large supermarket. For big families (over 9 persons) there may be a significant savings in buying from a wholesaler in carton lots. However, the savings for the average family would not compensate for the added time, inconvenience, need for storage space, and so forth. Cooperative buying arrangements based on purchases from a wholesaler are also likely to be impractical and cumbersome. Food-buying plans that require a purchaser to sign a contract for future purchases should be avoided.

Many people have accused the supermarkets, not only of contributing to inflation, but also of other "unfair practices," such as alluring decor, the playing of music, the presentation of a confusing number of items (sometimes 5,000) and the enticing display of nonfood items. Although these charges may be substantially correct, they seem trivial in contrast to the advantages offered by supermarkets. First, there is evidence that the supermarket buyers have actually helped keep prices down, by promoting substitutes for excessively priced foods. A large supermarket's profit margin on sales is usually less than 2%, a modest one in relation to the services performed for the buyer. The wide choice range from different manufacturers can be used advantageously by the careful shopper. Supermarket advertising of special purchases is hardly ever misleading—unlike, for example, the drug industry's. And last, supermarkets tend to be clean, and the food sold is usually wholesome and safe.

If the distance is not too great, you can plan to shop in two different supermarkets on a regular basis, and by comparison pricing you can save significantly—10 to 40% of your weekly food bill.

PLANNING WHAT TO BUY

A written list should be made out and taken along on each shopping trip. The list should be complete, but not too specific. For reasons that will become clear later, it would be better to list fruit, rather than apples, unless you happen to know the prices of the fruits beforehand. Substitutions may then be made freely if they will save money. Do not purchase items that are not on the list unless they offer a substantial savings. In this context, savings is not the same thing as a price reduction. For example, caviar might be reduced 50%, but its cost would still be high in relation to its nutritive value. In general, the "Food-Value Counter" in this book should be used as a guide as to whether a price reduction involves a true saving or not.

WHICH BRANDS TO BUY

A major function of the large supermarket chain is the screening of foods to be certain that they are of good quality, and you can be reasonably confident that the quality of foods you purchase there is high. Usually you can save money by buying the so-called private brands. These are the brands owned by the supermarket chain itself. For example, the Safeway brand is owned by the store of that name. Ann Page brand is owned by A & P, and so forth. Often, a large supermarket will own several private brands. The chain contracts with one of the companies that produces a well-known brand, and since they buy in enormous quantities, they get a discount which is passed on to the consumer. The private brands sold by the supermarket are actually produced in the same plants that make the nationally advertised brands, yet they are often better buys. There may be minor differences among various brands of the same food, but this is a matter of individual taste preference. The more expensive brands are not necessarily the best tasting. However, since one brand of canned fruit may have more syrup and less fruit than another, you will have to determine your true saving by trial and error in this case.

WHAT TO BUY—SOME GUIDELINES

In order to clarify the way in which a knowledge of comparative nutritional values can help save you money, we will compare several similar foods in some detail.*

Meat

There are several grades of meat. The most expensive is prime. Next come choice, good, standard, utility, cutter, and canner. All these grades are examined and graded by the U.S. Department of Agriculture and are equally safe. The difference among the grades is in the fat content. Prime meat has more fat than choice, which has more fat than good, and so on. The grades with more fat are generally softer and easier to cut and chew. The fat is not only the visible white fat that is usually trimmed off; *it is also present between the muscle fibers*. When present in large amounts, it gives a "marbled" appearance to the meat. As we have seen, the available evidence strongly points to beef fat as a major cause of heart attacks and arterial disease. It apparently stimulates cholesterol deposition. *When you pay high prices for top grades of meat, you are actually paying for something that in the long run is unhealthy*.

For example, after the beef cuts are trimmed to the retail level, choice grade, whole carcass, has 21% fat, good 19%, and standard 15%. The remainder is largely water and protein, since protein is usually present with large amounts of water in animal foods. Thus, a pound of choice porterhouse steak, as purchased, has 61 grams of protein and over 148 grams of fat.† A pound of choice sirloin steak has about 71 grams of protein and 112 grams of fat.

*Comparisons are based on prices in the Denver area during May and June of 1973.

†Composition of Foods. Agriculture Handbook No. 8, U.S. Department of Agriculture.

In general, the more expensive cuts tend to have more fat than the less expensive cuts within the same grade. (An exception is round steak which has less fat than protein, even in the choice grade.) Thus, it can be seen that it is not only more economical but healthier to buy the cheaper grades of meat. You can compensate for the increased toughness of the meat by using it for stews and hamburgers. Your major problem will be finding a store that sells the less fatty grades of beef, but if enough people ask supermarket managers to stock these grades (good, standard, and utility), some will probably do so.

Within a particular grade of meat, it is to your advantage to get the cuts with more protein and less fat, but prices are variable. For example, chuck steak, as cut, has slightly more protein per pound than T-bone of the same grade. Yet chuck steak was selling at $1.15 per pound and T-bone steak at $2.05 per pound in the same store at the same time. Although both cuts were overpriced, chuck steak was obviously the better buy. To determine which cut is the best buy at a particular price, consult the "Food-Value Counter" in this book.

Eggs

Eggs are labeled by grade and size. The grades are AA, A, and B. There is no difference in wholesomeness or nutritional value between these grades. The difference is in the appearance when the egg is cooked. A grade AA egg spreads out less than a grade B egg on the frying pan or poacher. Accordingly, whenever grade B eggs are cheaper, they are a better buy. Sizes of eggs are based on the weight per dozen. There is no nutritional difference between white and brown eggs. The official sizes are listed below.

Size	Weight per dozen
Jumbo	30 ounces
Extra large	27 ounces
Large	24 ounces
Medium	21 ounces
Small	18 ounces
Peewee	15 ounces

Usually the smaller eggs tend to be better buys. However, if the difference in price between two successive sizes is less than 8 cents, the larger of the two is a better buy.

Milk and Milk Products

Milk is available in several forms. Whole fresh milk is the most expensive and probably the least desirable. Although milk is indeed the best food for mammalian infants, it is by no means an ideal food for adolescents or adults. Whole milk contains substantial amounts of fat. Since milk is a dilute food, the fat content expressed as a percentage of the total doesn't seem high. It is 3.7%. However, in terms of the total caloric value, fat accounts for 39% of the calories in whole milk. If a person drank a quart of whole milk per day, the fat taken in would be about 37 grams, an undesirable amount for most people.

Skim fresh milk contains virtually no fat and is probably more healthful for most people. However, its price tends to be high.

Evaporated milk and condensed milk are modified by removal of water. Condensed milk is often sweetened by the addition of sugar. They are seldom drunk in large amounts and are useful in cooking and for addition to coffee.

Dried milk is available as dried whole milk and dried nonfat milk. The latter is superior for most purposes. Unfortunately, it sometimes has a metallic taste when reconstituted, and some people don't like to use it as a beverage. However, it is excellent for use in cooking.

Flour

In general, the thickeners most commonly used in cooking are cornstarch and flour. Cornstarch is cheap, but has no protein. Wheat flour is also cheap and contains protein, but sometimes it imparts a pasty flavor to food. Rye flour seems to be the best thickener for such foods as soups and sauces, since it does not add a strongly undesirable flavor. Rye flour is ordinarily more expensive than wheat flour. A pound of rye flour costs approximately 24¢, while wheat flour costs approximately 14¢ to 20¢. Nevertheless, the nutrient value of both flours is so high that at these prices both are good buys. The pound of rye flour contains 40 to 50 grams of protein, making it one of the most economical sources of protein. Two level tablespoons of rye flour added to a serving of soup improves the flavor and more than doubles the protein content at low cost.

Bread

The nutrient content of different breads is quite close, seldom differing by more than 25% in protein content or by more than 20% in total caloric value. Accordingly, the value of breads is also quite close. Some breads cost more than their nutrient content justifies, but if one desires variety, even these breads are still good buys for overall nutritional value. On the other hand, breads that are more expensive because they have such additives as butter, eggs, or honey, may not necessarily be significantly more nutritious. The nutrient value of butter is probably negative, the nutrient value of honey is basically the same as that of sugar, and the nutrient value of the egg is dependent on how much is added.

Potatoes and Rice

Potatoes and rice are common foods used to add starch and small amounts of protein to a meal. If potatoes cost 15¢ per pound, and long grain rice costs 22¢ per pound at a particular time, one might think that potatoes are a better buy. However, a pound of potatoes contains about 8 grams of protein and 63 grams of carbohydrate, while a pound of long grain rice as purchased contains 33 grams of protein and 368 grams of carbohydrate. (Potatoes have some vitamin C but much of this is lost in mashing.) In effect, a pound of long grain rice (not instant) has between 4 and 6 times the nutritional value of a pound of potatoes. Accordingly, at these prices, rice is a much better buy than potatoes.

Sugar and Sugar Products

White and brown sugar

The nutritional value of white and brown sugar is almost identical. White sugar has approximately 451 grams of pure sugar per pound, while brown sugar has about 437 grams of sugar per pound. Neither has any protein or fat. Brown sugar has small amounts of calcium and iron, but since people don't eat anything like a pound of sugar per day, these minerals are of little nutritional significance. If one were to evaluate the true value of the calcium, iron, and trace minerals in brown sugar, it would probably be well under 1¢ per pound. Nevertheless, at the same time in the same store, white sugar cost 11¢ per pound, while brown sugar cost 18½¢ per pound, about 2/3 more. Since there is no scientific support for the notion that brown sugar is healthier than white, there is no reason to pay an inflated price for it. Honey is also vastly overpriced in relation to its nutritional value.

Sugar and syrups

Syrups, as used on pancakes and waffles, are basically a solution of sugar in water, sometimes with coloring and flavoring, artificial or natural. But in the same store on the same day, the price of pure granulated sugar was 11¢ per pound, while the price of syrups ranged from 34¢ to 38¢ per pound, and this includes the water. Molasses, which is a mixture of sugar, water, impurities, and incidental dirt cost about 50¢ per pound. Clearly, syrups and molasses are priced far over their true nutritional value, and there is no need to pay such high prices for these products. One can produce the equivalent much more cheaply at home, following the recipe in this book.

Types of Corn

The corn eaten as a table vegetable is quite a different variety from the corn used to make cornmeal and corn products. The latter is referred to as field corn. Field corn contains more than twice as much protein, fat, and carbohydrate as an equivalent amount of sweet corn. However, field corn does not have the flavor or texture that would make it suitable as a table vegetable.

Beans—Dried, Canned, and Frozen

Dry beans are among the best buys by a wide margin. However, they must be cooked and some sort of sauce added. Canned beans cost about the same per pound as dry beans, but their weight includes a great deal of water. Their nutritional value is about 1/3 as much as dry beans, so, in effect, they cost three times as much for the nutrients. On the other hand, they offer greater convenience, for example as a quick lunch. In other situations, dry beans, pressure cooked, are the best choice.

Frozen green beans cost 24¢ for 9 ounces, and frozen lima beans cost 28¢ for 10 ounces. Translated into pounds, this comes to 43¢ per pound for green beans and 45¢ for lima beans. Superficially, this might seem as if green beans were a slightly better buy. However, if we analyze their nutritional value, a different picture emerges. A pound of frozen lima beans contains 34 grams of protein, 104 grams of carbohydrate, and 85 milligrams of ascorbic acid (vitamin C). Comparatively, a pound of frozen green beans contains only 7 grams of protein, 28 grams of carbohydrate, and 45 milligrams of ascorbic acid. Green beans contain slightly more vitamin A than lima beans, but neither is a major source of this vitamin. In nutritional terms, a pound of frozen lima beans is worth from 2 to 4 times as much as a pound of frozen green beans, and, accordingly, they are a far better buy at current prices.

Carrots and Acorn Squash

I have chosen these two vegetables because they both have important amounts of vitamin A. Each has a small amount of other nutrients, which would be largely insignificant in one's total daily food intake. By that, I mean that a usual serving of either vegetable would provide less than 5% of the daily intake of any nutrient other than vitamin A, and probably less than 2% of the daily intake of all other nutrients. Each, however, would provide a significant amount of vitamin A. A pound of acorn squash provides slightly over 4,000 units of vitamin A. By comparison, a pound of carrots provides over 30,000 units of vitamin A, more than 7 times as much. Nevertheless, a pound of carrots cost 15¢ to 19½¢ while a pound of acorn squash cost 33¢. Clearly, carrots are a much better buy than acorn squash at these prices.

Yellow and Red Onions

There is no important nutritional difference between yellow and red onions. Nevertheless, on the same day in the same store, yellow onions were selling at 21¢ per pound, and red onions at 59¢ per pound. Obviously, yellow onions were the better buy, and one wonders why people bought the red onions.

Bananas and Apples

Both bananas and apples are common and popular fruits. Bananas have more of all significant nutrients than apples, including protein, carbohydrate, and ascorbic acid. Nevertheless, bananas were 15¢ to 17¢ per pound, while apples were 39¢ per pound, more than twice as much. At such prices, bananas are a much better buy.

Lettuce and Cabbage

Lettuce and cabbage are both leafy vegetables that may be eaten raw, and that are tasty in salads. But in a per pound comparison, cabbage contains about 5 grams of protein, lettuce about 3½; cabbage has approximately 20 grams of carbohydrate, lettuce 12; and cabbage contains about 170 milligrams of ascorbic acid, while lettuce has only about 25. Lettuce has more vitamin A than some varieties of cabbage and less than others, but neither vegetable is an important source of this vitamin. Cabbage is a better buy nutritionally than lettuce, even if they cost the same.

Coffee and Coffee Lighteners

Coffees cannot be compared for nutritional value, since they have none. They are consumed for taste, and for the effect of the caffeine in them. Extensive and expensive advertising tries to convince people that one brand is better than another. We have found, however, that the private supermarket brands are unsurpassed for flavor, and considerably cheaper than the nationally advertised brands.

In the past, cream was commonly added to coffee to improve its flavor and to lighten its color. Then, nondairy additives were introduced. Unfortunately, some contain coconut oil. Others are quite expensive for their nutrient value. The best material to use is dry nonfat milk. Three to four level teaspoonsful of the dry powder added to a cup of coffee improves the taste as much as any other material, but is much less expensive and much more nutritious. It is 36% protein, so that 4 teaspoonsful provides a significant amount of this nutrient.

STOCKING AND STORING OF FOODS

Stocking Dried Goods

Stocking up on meats and other high-priced foods may not result in any savings, since one is then likely to eat more of the expensive foods. It is, however, a good idea to stock up on inexpensive staples. If the current situation worsens, these staples may become unobtainable, or their prices may skyrocket. In the event of any type of disaster, a supply of staples can protect a family against malnutrition. Even if nothing serious happens, a good stock of staples will help reduce food costs because of the tendency to use what is at hand. In general, for a family of four, a stock of staples should include 20 pounds of flour, 20 pounds of cornmeal and oatmeal, 20 pounds of sugar, 20 pounds of dried macaroni and spaghetti, and 40 pounds of dried beans of several kinds. All this would cost about $20 to $30, and would provide food for four at emergency levels for a month. These staples should be used and stocks gradually replenished, so that the stored items are not kept more than six months. They can be purchased gradually so as not to disrupt the currently volatile supply and demand situation. The date of purchase should be written on each container and package.

Home Freezers

A home freezer is a convenience, but seldom a means of saving on the cost of food. If a freezer is purchased outright for cash, without any so-called "easy payments" or the need for any borrowing, the true costs of keeping food frozen in it range from 22¢ to 28¢ per pound per year. These costs include electricity, depreciation, insurance, and so forth. If a freezer is purchased on so-called easy payments, or on money borrowed from a lending institution at the usual interest rate of 18% per year, the true cost of keeping food in it is much higher, perhaps 40¢ to 45¢ per pound per year. It is rarely, if ever, possible to save this sort of money by buying at sales and freezing the food, so buying a home freezer with credit or a loan should be looked upon as unwise for most families.

The purchase of a home freezer for cash without borrowing may or may not provide savings in food costs, depending on how the freezer is used. Let us assume that one buys food at a sale and keeps it an average of six months before eating it. The storage for 6 months costs 11¢ to 14¢ per pound, so at first glance it might seem as though one can save by this method, provided the food on sale costs at least 15¢ per pound less than the usual cost. However, this would only be true if the availability of the freezer does not change the amount of various foods that are eaten. For example, let us consider a family that would ordinarily eat a total of 10 pounds of beef per week at an average cost of $1.25 per pound. Let us assume that at a sale the beef cut that they usually buy is reduced to 95¢ a pound, and that they buy 50 pounds which is stored in their freezer. If they continue to consume 10 pounds of beef per week, then they will have saved some money by stocking their freezer. However, if the presence of the large amount of beef induces them to increase their consumption to 14 or 15 pounds per week, there will be no savings, and even a substantial additional cost for the family food. If one seriously intends to save on the food budget, the proportion of expensive foods eaten each week should not be increased because of sales, or storage of reduced price meat in the freezer.

Chapter 3

THE FOOD-VALUE COUNTER
AND HOW TO USE IT

METHOD USED TO DETERMINE THE FAIR
VALUE OF NUTRIENTS IN FOOD

The Food-Value Counter is designed to help you obtain maximum nutrition at fair cost. The calculations were obtained by computer, and although based on the prices in large food chains in May and June 1973, the nutritional values will stay in the same proportions, even if food prices change over a fairly wide range.

First, the value of fat was determined. Four types of unsaturated oils, corn, safflower, soybean, and cottonseed, were quite close in price—varying less than 5%. These oils are about the healthiest available. The average price of these oils was then calculated, and it came to approximately 46¢ per pound, or about 0.1¢ per gram. This was then used as the fair value of fats and oils.

Next, the price values of the major carbohydrate-containing foods were considered. Only basic foods that provided at least 70% of their calories as carbohydrate were included. They were sugar, bread, potatoes, spaghetti, corn meal, dry beans, cream of wheat, and rice. The small amounts of fat in these foods were credited at the previously determined value of 0.1¢ per gram of fat. The protein in these foods was given a tentative correction value, to be checked later against high protein foods. The average cost of the carbohydrate in the eight major foods was 0.045¢ per gram. This was then used as the fair value of carbohydrates.

Next, the prices of the major foods containing relatively high amounts of protein were considered. Animal protein levels had to be at least 55 grams per pound, and vegetable protein levels had to be at least 110 grams per pound for inclusion. (There are approximately 454 grams in a pound.) The foods included were chicken, beef (hamburger), salmon (canned), dry nonfat milk, cottage cheese and peanut butter. The fat and carbohydrate content of these foods was credited at 0.1¢ per gram and 0.045¢ per gram respectively. The average value of the protein in these foods came to 0.71¢ per gram. This was then used as the fair value of protein.

Finally, the values assigned to fat and carbohydrate were compared. Since both these nutrients are utilized primarily for energy, their relative values should be close to the proportion which their caloric values bear to each other. Since a gram of fat provides 9.3 calories and a gram of carbohydrate provides 4.1 calories, their relative values should be close to 9.3/4.1 (2.27). A variation of up to 10% was initially considered the maximum allowable. Actually, the ratio of the assigned values, 0.1/0.045, turned out to be 2.22, which is less than 3% away from the theoretical ratio. Accordingly, it appears that the method used to calculate the value of the basic nutrients is reasonable.

These values were then checked for internal consistency. Any reasonable change in the value of protein tentatively credited to those high carbohydrate foods that also had some protein did not alter the assigned carbohydrate value by more than 5%. Similarly, any reasonable change in the value of carbohydrate or fat credited to those high protein foods that also had carbohydrate or fat did not alter the assigned protein value by more than 5%.

HOW TO USE THE FOOD-VALUE COUNTER

In essence, this counter is based on assigning a dollar and cents value to each major nutrient, with an additional increment for substantial amounts of vitamins, roughage, value in seasoning, and preparation costs.

Although some of the following explanation may seem rather complex, the Food-Value Counter itself is quite simple. The complexities have been taken care of by the computer, and one can get all the information needed for thrifty shopping just by referring to column 7. After one day or so, it will be quite easy to use the Counter to save a lot of money. For easy reference, the food items and column 7 (fair value range) of the Food Value Counter have been reproduced at the end of the book (pp. 159–177) so that you can remove pages and take them with you for handy reference at the supermarket.

The figures in columns 5, 6, and 7 are expressed in cents per pound. The total value range per pound is given in column 7. The range has been obtained by using the sum of columns 5 and 6 as the minimum, and a 25 percent increase as the maximum. This provides for variations in quality. The figures in column 7 can be used to judge the relative value of different foods, and to guide your purchases. The estimated value of the major nutrients per pound is listed in column 5. In columns 2, 3, and 4, the amounts of protein, fat, and carbohydrate in grams per pound are listed. The increments for vitamins, roughage, seasoning effect, and preparation costs are listed in column 6.

In general, although the costs as calculated for this table as "Fair value range per pound" will vary considerably in the course of time, their nutritional values will stay in the same proportions. Even if food prices change, the Counter can still serve as a guide. For example, if food A is listed in column 7 as having a value of 20 to 25¢ per pound, and food B is listed as having a value of 40 to 50¢ per pound, one may deduce that food B is worth roughly twice as much as food A. If at a particular time, food A is selling at 28¢ a pound, and food B at 42¢ a pound, food B is the better buy. Conversely, if food A is selling at 18¢ a pound and food B at 50¢ a pound, food A is a better buy. In general, one can assume that any food selling within the range in column 7 is a good buy, any food selling at a lower price is a bargain, and a food selling at a price over the range in column 7 can be considered expensive. Unfortunately, many foods—such as meat and fish—are already selling at much higher prices than the values listed in column 7. If one is going to buy these foods, one can still use column 7 as a guide to find out which food is relatively less overpriced. Within a particular classification group such as meats, poultry, and fish, one can compare prices directly, without bothering with percentages. This approximation is good enough for practical purposes. For example, if meat cut A is listed in column 7 as having a value of 60 to 70¢ a pound, and is selling at $1.49, the difference between $1.49 and 70¢ is 79¢, the extent to which it is overpriced. If meat cut B is listed as 70 to 80¢ and it is selling at $1.55 a pound, cut B is overpriced by 75¢. Cut B, then, is a better buy if one intends to buy meat.

The values assigned to the major nutrients are 0.71¢ per gram for animal protein, 0.1¢ per gram for fat, and 0.045¢ per gram for carbohydrate. For plant protein, the value assigned per gram is half of the value assigned for animal protein. This is based on the fact that plant proteins have lower indices of digestibility, and lower biological values. Also, this figure applies when the plant protein is eaten as the sole source of protein during a particular meal, without any complementary protein. Of course, this seldom happens, so that the values for plant protein are, if anything, understated. If you eat two or more plant proteins (including grains) at a meal, you will get a greater value than that presented in column 7.

The increment for vitamins is arbitrarily assigned as a maximum of 5¢ per pound for most foods that contain a large amount of vitamins, and lesser values for foods with less vitamins. For a few foods that contain enormous amounts of vitamins, increments over 5¢ per pound are added. It is impractical to attempt to assign precise values to vitamins.

The value for roughage is assigned as a maximum of 5¢ per pound. Here, too, assignment of precise values is impractical.

Value for seasoning effect is based on ability of a seasoning agent to improve the taste of low-priced foods, since this ability can result indirectly in considerable savings. For example, raisins are useful in flavoring puddings and desserts made with such low-cost foods as flour, and nonfat dry milk. Without the raisins or something similar, the pudding or dessert might be so tasteless that it wouldn't be eaten. Similarly, garlic, onions, celery, and tomatoes can be used to improve the flavor of casserole dishes and meat extenders. Therefore, they have a value beyond their nutrient content. In general, this added value is calculated on the basis of the amount of low-priced food that is made more tasty by addition of the flavoring food. It takes quite a bit of tomato to flavor a casserole, compared to the amount of vanilla extract needed to flavor a pudding or cake. Therefore, the vanilla extract would be assigned a higher value. On the other hand, condiments such as steak sauce are used almost entirely to improve the taste of expensive foods. They would, therefore, be assigned little or no value.

The final reason for adding to the value of a food is preparation saving. For some foods, the labor of preparation is such that it is impractical for most people. For example, although the nutrient value of a pound of bread is less than the nutrient value of a pound of flour (because bread contains more water), people don't usually eat plain flour,* and it takes too long to bake bread. Furthermore, the baking, slicing, and packaging are all done by the bakery so that the consumer need only eat the bread. Surely this service has substantial value, and I assign to it up to 10¢ per pound in the prepared food. Lesser amounts are assigned to foods that save less home preparation. The so-called convenience foods, such as TV dinners, are in a similar category.

Canned foods are usually assigned an increment of 5¢ per pound because of the storage as well as preparation convenience involved. However, if you buy some canned food, intending to eat it within a day or so, the increment may not be worth 5¢ per pound to you. In that case, you can readily adjust the fair value range (column 7) for your own needs.

Certain correction factors have been included in the calculations. Some foods are high in saturated fat. There is, as pointed out in chapter 1, convincing evidence that saturated fats in substantial amounts are harmful. It hardly makes sense to assign a positive monetary value to an ingredient that can cause

*Plain flour can be eaten in an emergency, and it is nutritious.

severe illness and even death. On the other hand, small amounts of saturated fat are probably not harmful, and have nutritional value. Therefore, the computer providing the figure for value of major nutrients was programmed to give full value to saturated fats up to 10% of the weight of the food (45.4 grams per pound), but to give no value to saturated fat after the 45.4 gram amount is exceeded. For unsaturated fat, the full value is given, without a ceiling.

For some goods, such as cakes, there is no way of telling whether saturated or unsaturated fats are used. The calculation is for unsaturated fats. If you find that a particular cake is made with saturated fat, deduct a few cents from the fair value range.

A few foods, notably brains, are probably undesirable in any quantity because of high cholesterol levels. These foods are given zero value in the table.

You will note that while some foods are bargains, and some are reasonably priced, some are priced way over the fair value range. This doesn't mean that you must eliminate the overpriced foods entirely. You should reduce their use, both in amount per serving and in servings per week. At the same time, increase the use of bargain and reasonably priced food. This will provide balanced, nutritious, tasty meals at considerable savings.

It is significant that there are still many foods that are real bargains. These include grains, flours, breads, beans, some vegetables and fruits, some milk products, some cheeses, and sugar. By increasing the use of these foods, a great deal can be saved.

FOOD VALUE COUNTER

FOOD VALUE COUNTER

1	2	3	4	5	6	7
Food	Protein gm/lb.	Fat gm/lb.	Carbo-hydrate gm/lb.	Value of major nutrients per pound	Increments for vitamins, rough-age, seasoning effect and preparation	Fair value range per pound as purchased
almonds, dried						
in shell	43.0	125.4	45.1	30	3+1+3+0	37-46
shelled	84.4	245.9	88.5	59	5+2+5+3	74-93
anchovy	87.1	46.7	1.4	66	0+0+4+5	75-94
apples						
dried, sulfured	4.5	7.3	325.7	17	0+5+5+2	29-36
fresh, good quality	.8	2.5	60.5	3	2+5+3+0	13-16
frozen, sweetened	.9	.5	110.2	5	2+5+3+0	15-19
apple butter	1.8	3.6	212.3	11	1+5+5+3	25-31
apple juice, canned or bottled	.5	.1	54.0	3	0+0+0+5	8-10
applesauce, canned						
sweetened	.9	.5	108.0	5	0+3+0+5	13-16
unsweetened	.9	.9	49.0	3	0+3+0+5	11-14
apricots						
canned, light sirup pack	3.2	.5	76.2	5	4+4+4+5	22-28
dried, sulfured	22.7	2.3	301.6	22	5+5+5+4	41-51
frozen, sweetened	3.2	.5	113.9	6	4+4+4+0	18-23
raw	4.3	.9	54.6	4	5+5+4+0	18-23
apricot nectar, canned	1.4	.5	66.2	4	2+2+0+4	12-15
asparagus						
canned, spears, green	8.6	1.4	13.2	4	5+5+0+5	19-24
frozen, cuts and tips	15.0	.9	16.3	6	5+5+0+0	16-20
raw, spears	6.4	.5	12.7	3	5+5+0+0	13-16

avocados, raw, all commercial varieties	7.1	55.8	21.4	9	5+5+0+0	19-24
bacon						
Canadian, unheated	90.7	65.3	1.4	69	4+0+0+0	73-91
cured, sliced, raw	38.1	314.3	4.5	32	2+0+0+0	34-43
bananas, raw, good quality	3.4	.6	68.5	4	3+5+3+0	15-19
barley, pearled, light	37.2	4.5	357.4	43	3+1+0+0	47-59
bass						
smallmouth and largemouth, raw, whole	26.6	3.7	0	19	0+1+0+0	20-25
striped, raw, whole	36.9	5.3	0	27	0+1+0+0	28-35
beans, common, mature seeds, dry						
white						
canned						
with pork and sweet sauce	28.1	21.3	95.7	16	0+2+0+5	23-29
with pork and tomato sauce	27.7	11.8	86.2	15	0+2+0+5	22-28
without pork	28.6	2.3	104.3	15	0+2+0+5	22-28
raw	101.2	7.3	278.1	49	0+2+0+0	51-64
red						
canned, with solids and liquid	25.9	1.8	74.4	13	0+1+0+5	19-24
raw	102.1	6.8	280.8	50	0+2+0+0	52-65
pinto, calico, red Mexican, raw	103.9	5.4	288.9	51	0+2+0+0	53-66
other, including black, brown, and Bayo, raw	101.2	6.8	277.6	49	0+2+0+0	51-64
beans, lima						
canned, regular pack	18.6	1.4	60.8	10	3+3+0+5	21-26
frozen						
baby limas	34.5	.9	104.3	17	5+3+0+0	25-31
Fordhooks	28.1	.5	88.5	14	5+4+0+0	23-29
immature seeds, raw						
in pod	15.2	.9	40.1	7	3+3+0+0	13-16
shelled	38.1	2.3	100.2	18	5+5+0+0	28-35
mature seeds, dry, raw	92.5	7.3	290.3	47	1+1+0+0	49-61

1	2	3	4	5	6	7
Food	Protein gm/lb.	Fat gm/lb.	Carbo-hydrate gm/lb.	Value of major nutrients per pound	Increments for vitamins, rough-age, seasoning effect and preparation	Fair value range per pound as purchased
beans, snap						
green						
canned, regular pack	4.5	.5	19.1	2	2+3+0+5	12-15
frozen, cut	7.7	.5	27.2	4	5+5+0+0	14-18
raw	7.6	.8	28.3	4	5+5+0+0	14-18
yellow, or wax, raw	6.8	.8	24.0	4	5+5+0+0	14-18
beans and frankfurters, canned	34.5	32.2	57.2	30	0+1+0+5	36-45
beef						
chuck cuts, choice grade						
arm						
with bone	78.8	62.9	0	60	5+0+0+0	65-81
without bone	88.0	70.3	0	67	5+0+0+0	72-90
entire chuck						
with bone	71.6	75.0	0	55	5+0+0+0	60-75
without bone	84.8	88.9	0	69	5+0+0+0	74-93
rib, 5th						
with bone	62.1	120.4	0	49	5+0+0+0	54-68
without bone	73.5	142.4	0	57	5+0+0+0	62-78
flank steak, choice grade	98.0	25.9	0	72	5+0+0+0	77-96
hamburger, raw						
lean	93.9	45.4	0	71	5+0+0+0	76-95
regular	81.2	96.2	0	62	5+0+0+0	67-84
hindshank, choice grade						
with bone	38.1	48.9	0	32	5+0+0+0	37-46
without bone	82.6	106.1	0	63	5+0+0+0	68-85
loin or short loin, choice gr.						
club steak	58.9	132.1	0	46	5+0+0+0	51-64
porterhouse steak	60.8	148.8	0	48	5+0+0+0	53-66
T-bone steak	59.1	149.1	0	46	5+0+0+0	51-64

loin end or sirloin, choice gr.					
double-bone sirloin steak					
with bone	61.1	108.4	0	48	5+0+0+0	53-66
without bone	74.4	132.0	0	57	5+0+0+0	62-78
hipbone sirloin steak					
with bone	55.8	149.3	0	44	5+0+0+0	49-61
without bone	65.8	176.0	0	51	5+0+0+0	56-70
wedge and round-bone sirloin					
with bone	71.1	112.3	0	55	5+0+0+0	60-75
without bone	76.7	121.1	0	59	5+0+0+0	64-80
rib, choice grade					
entire rib, 6-12th ribs					
with bone	61.8	156.1	0	48	5+0+0+0	53-66
without bone	67.1	169.6	0	52	5+0+0+0	57-71
rib, 6th or blade					
with bone	67.1	137.2	0	52	5+0+0+0	57-71
without bone	72.6	148.3	0	56	5+0+0+0	61-76
ribs, 11th-12th					
with bone	56.9	177.2	0	45	5+0+0+0	50-63
without bone	62.1	193.7	0	49	5+0+0+0	54-68
round, entire, choice grade					
with bone	88.5	53.9	0	67	5+0+0+0	72-90
without bone	91.6	55.8	0	69	5+0+0+0	74-93
rump, choice grade					
with bone	67.0	97.4	0	52	5+0+0+0	57-71
without bone	78.9	114.8	0	60	5+0+0+0	65-81
short plate, choice grade					
with bone	59.7	150.6	0	47	5+0+0+0	52-65
without bone	67.1	169.2	0	52	5+0+0+0	57-71
beef and vegetable stew, canned	26.3	14.1	32.2	22	3+2+0+5	32-40
beef, canned, roast beef	113.0	59.0	0	85	5+0+0+5	95-119
beef, corned, boneless					
canned, medium-fat	114.8	54.0	0	86	5+0+0+5	96-120
uncooked, medium-fat	71.7	113.0	0	55	5+0+0+0	60-75
beef, dried, chipped	155.6	28.6	0	113	5+0+0+5	123-154

1	2	3	4	5	6	7
Food	Protein gm/lb.	Fat gm/lb.	Carbo-hydrate gm/lb.	Value of major nutrients per pound	Increments for vitamins, rough-age, seasoning effect and preparation	Fair value range per pound as purchased
beef potpie, frozen	33.1	44.9	81.6	32	2+0+5	39-49
beets, common, red canned, regular pack raw, without tops	4.1 5.1	.5 .3	35.8 31.4	3 3	3+5+0+5 3+5+0+0	16-20 11-14
beet greens, common, raw	5.6	.8	11.7	3	5+5+0+0	13-16
biscuits, baking powder, made from home-style recipe with enriched flour	33.6	77.1	207.7	29	2+0+0+10	41-51
biscuit dough, with enriched flour, frozen	25.9	54.0	221.8	25	2+0+0+5	32-40
biscuit mix, enriched flour, dry form	34.9	57.2	311.6	32	2+0+0+3	37-46
blackberries, including dew-berries, boysenberries, youngberries, raw	5.2	3.9	55.6	5	5+5+3+0	18-23
blackberries, canned, heavy sirup	3.6	2.7	100.7	6	2+3+2+5	18-23
blackberry juice, canned unsweetened	1.4	2.7	35.4	2	3+0+0+5	10-13
blueberries frozen, unsweetened raw	3.2 2.9	2.3 2.1	61.7 63.8	4 4	3+5+2+0 3+5+2+0	14-18 14-18

34

bluefish, raw, whole	47.4	7.6	0	34	5+0+0+0	39-49
Boston brown bread	24.9	5.9	206.8	19	2+1+0+10	32-40
brains, all kinds, raw	47.2	39.0	3.6	0	0+0+0+0	0
bran, added sugar and malt extract	57.2	13.6	337.0	37	5+5+0+5	52-65
bran flakes						
40% bran	46.3	8.2	365.6	34	5+5+0+5	49-61
with raisins	37.6	6.4	359.7	31	5+5+0+5	46-58
brazilnuts						
in shell	31.1	145.6	23.7	27	1+2+0+0	30-38
shelled	64.9	303.5	49.4	56	2+3+0+2	63-79
bread						
cracked wheat	39.5	10.0	236.3	26	5+2+0+10	43-54
French or Vienna, enriched flour	41.3	13.6	251.3	28	5+2+0+10	45-56
Italian, enriched flour	41.3	3.6	255.8	27	5+2+0+10	44-55
raisin	29.9	12.7	243.1	23	5+2+0+10	40-50
rye						
American	41.3	5.0	236.3	26	5+2+0+10	43-54
pumpernickel	41.3	5.4	240.9	26	5+2+0+10	43-54
salt-rising	35.8	10.9	236.8	25	5+2+0+10	42-53
white, enriched, made with 1%-2% nonfat dry milk	39.5	14.5	228.6	26	5+2+0+10	43-54
whole-wheat, made with 2% nonfat dry milk	47.6	13.6	216.4	28	5+2+0+10	45-56
water	41.3	11.8	223.6	26	5+2+0+10	43-54
breadcrumbs, dry, grated	57.2	20.9	332.9	38	5+2+0+10	55-69
broccoli						
frozen, chopped	14.5	1.4	23.6	6	5+5+2+2	20-25
raw, partially trimmed	12.7	1.1	20.9	6	5+5+2+0	18-23

1	2	3	4	5	6	7
Food	Protein gm/lb.	Fat gm/lb.	Carbohydrate gm/lb.	Value of major nutrients per pound	Increments for vitamins, roughage, seasoning effect and preparation	Fair value range per pound as purchased
brussels sprouts, raw, good quality	20.4	1.7	34.6	9	5+5+5+0	19-24
buckwheat flour, dark	53.1	11.3	326.6	35	5+1+0+0	41-51
butter	2.7	367.0	1.8	6	5+0+0+0	11-14
butterfish, northern, raw	41.9	23.6	0	32	0+0+0+0	32-40
buttermilk, fluid, cultured	16.3	.5	23.1	13	1+0+0+0	14-18
butternuts						
in shell	15.1	38.9	5.3	9	0+2+0+0	11-14
shelled	107.5	277.6	38.1	68	0+3+0+3	74-93
cabbage, common varieties						
dehydrated	56.2	7.7	334.3	36	5+5+8+5	59-74
raw, head trimmed	5.3	.8	22.0	3	5+5+5+0	18-23
cakes made from home-type recipe						
angelfood	32.2	.9	273.1	24	2+0+0+10	36-45
Boston cream pie	22.7	42.6	226.3	23	2+0+0+10	35-44
most	20.4	74.4	253.1	24	2+0+0+10	36-45
cake mix						
angelfood	38.1	.9	401.4	32	2+0+0+5	39-49
most	20.0	39.5	281.2	24	2+0+0+5	31-39
candy						
caramels, plain or chocolate	18.1	46.3	347.5	27	0+0+0+5	32-40
chocolate, milk						
plain	34.9	146.5	258.1	39	0+0+0+5	44-55
with almonds	42.2	161.5	232.7	42	1+0+0+5	48-60
with peanuts	64.0	172.8	202.3	49	4+0+0+5	58-73

chocolate, sweet	20.0	159.2	262.6	35	0+0+0+5	40-50
chocolate-coated						
peanuts	74.4	187.3	177.4	53	4+0+0+5	62-78
raisins	24.5	77.6	319.8	31	0+0+0+5	36-45
hard	0	5.0	440.9	21	0+0+0+5	26-33
jelly beans	0	2.3	422.3	20	0+0+0+5	25-31
marshmallows	9.1	0	364.7	20	0+0+0+5	25-31
peanut bars	79.4	146.1	214.1	53	5+0+0+5	63-79
peanut brittle	25.9	47.2	367.4	31	2+0+0+5	38-48
carp, raw, whole	24.5	5.7	0	18	5+0+0+0	23-29
carrots						
canned, regular pack	2.7	.9	29.5	2	8+5+1+5	21-26
raw, without tops	4.1	.7	36.1	3	10+5+1+0	19-24
cashew nuts	78.0	207.3	132.9	54	4+2+0+1	61-76
catfish, freshwater, fillets, raw	79.8	14.1	0	58	5+0+0+3	66-83
cauliflower, raw, fully trimmed	12.2	.9	23.6	6	5+5+2+0	18-23
celery, all varieties	3.1	.3	13.3	2	3+5+4+0	14-18
chard, swiss, raw, good quality	10.0	1.3	19.2	5	5+5+1+0	16-20
cheeses						
natural cheeses						
blue or roquefort type	97.5	138.3	9.1	74	4+0+0+5	83-104
brick	100.7	138.3	8.6	76	4+0+0+5	85-106
camembert (domestic)	79.4	112.0	8.2	61	4+0+0+5	70-88
cheddar (American)	113.4	146.1	9.5	85	4+0+5+5	99-124
cottage cheese, creamed	61.7	19.1	13.2	46	3+0+0+5	54-68
cottage cheese, uncreamed	77.1	1.4	12.2	55	3+0+0+5	63-79
cream	36.3	171.0	9.5	31	3+0+0+5	39-49
limburger	96.2	127.0	10.0	73	4+0+0+5	82-103
parmesan	163.3	117.9	13.2	121	5+0+5+5	136-170
Swiss (domestic)	124.7	127.0	7.7	93	4+0+0+5	102-128

Food	Protein gm/lb.	Fat gm/lb.	Carbo- hydrate gm/lb.	Value of major nutrients per pound	Increments for vitamins, rough- age, seasoning effect and preparation	Fair value range per pound as purchased
	2	3	4	5	6	7
cheeses (cont.)						
pasteurized process						
American	105.2	136.1	8.6	79	5+0+5+5	94-118
cheese food (American)	89.8	108.9	32.2	70	5+0+5+5	85-106
cheese spread (American)	72.6	97.1	37.2	58	5+0+0+5	68-85
pimento (American)	104.3	137.0	8.2	79	5+0+5+5	94-118
Swiss	119.8	122.0	7.3	90	5+0+0+5	100-125
cherries						
canned, red, heavy sirup						
sour, without pits	3.6	.9	103.0	6	4+5+0+5	20-25
sweet	3.9	.9	88.3	6	4+5+0+5	20-25
frozen, sour, red, unsweetened	4.5	1.8	60.8	5	4+5+5+0	19-24
raw, sweet	5.3	1.2	71.0	5	4+5+0+0	14-18
chicken, raw						
fryers, ready-to-cook	57.4	15.1	0	42	5+0+0+2	49-61
cut-up parts						
back	40.4	23.5	0	31	5+0+0+2	38-48
breast	74.5	8.6	0	54	5+0+0+2	61-76
drumstick	51.2	10.6	0	37	5+0+0+2	44-55
neck	33.7	20.5	0	26	5+0+0+2	33-41
thigh	61.6	19.1	0	46	5+0+0+2	53-66
wing	41.1	16.5	0	31	5+0+0+2	38-48
roasters, ready-to-cook	60.3	59.3	0	49	5+0+0+0	54-68
hens and cocks, ready-to-cook	57.6	82.1	0	49	5+0+0+0	54-68
chicken, canned, meat only, boned	98.4	53.1	0	75	5+0+0+10	90-113
chicken potpie, frozen	30.4	52.2	100.7	31	4+1+0+5	41-51
chickpeas or garbanzos, mature seeds, dry, raw	93.0	21.8	276.7	48	3+1+0+0	51-65

38

Food					
chickory, witloof, raw	4.0	.4	12.9	2	0+5+1+0	8-10
chili con carne, canned						
with beans	34.0	27.7	55.3	29	2+2+0+5	38-48
without beans	46.7	67.1	26.3	41	2+2+0+5	50-63
chocolate, bitter or baking	48.5	240.4	131.1	47	1+0+10+0	58-73
chocolate sirup						
fudge type	23.1	62.1	244.9	26	0+0+5+0	31-39
thin type	10.4	9.1	284.4	18	0+0+10+0	28-35
chop suey with meat, canned	20.0	14.5	19.1	9	2+0+0+5	16-20
chow mein with chicken, canned	11.8	.5	32.2	6	2+0+0+5	13-16
clams, raw, hard or round						
meat and liquid in shell	9.4	.6	6.1	7	3+0+5+0	15-19
cocoa and chocolate flavored						
beverage powders						
with nonfat dry milk	84.4	13.2	321.1	46	2+0+2+3	53-66
without milk	18.1	9.1	405.5	26	2+0+5+0	33-41
mix for hot chocolate	42.6	48.1	335.2	35	2+0+0+5	42-53
cod						
dried, salted	131.5	3.2	0	94	5+0+3+5	107-134
raw, flesh only	79.8	1.4	0	57	5+0+0+5	67-84
collards, leaves without						
stems, raw	14.8	2.5	23.1	7	10+5+0+0	22-28
cookies						
assorted, packaged	23.1	91.6	322.1	32	2+0+0+10	44-55
fig bars	17.7	25.4	342.0	25	2+5+0+10	42-53
oatmeal with raisins	28.1	69.9	333.4	32	2+5+0+10	49-61
peanut	45.4	86.6	303.9	39	5+2+0+10	56-70
raisin	20.0	24.0	366.5	26	2+3+0+10	41-51
sandwich type	21.8	102.1	314.3	32	2+0+0+10	44-55
sugar wafers	22.2	88.0	332.9	32	2+0+0+10	44-55
vanilla wafers	24.5	73.0	337.5	32	2+0+0+10	44-55

Food	Protein gm/lb.	Fat gm/lb.	Carbohydrate gm/lb.	Value of major nutrients per pound	Increments for vitamins, roughage, seasoning effect and preparation	Fair value range per pound as purchased
cookie mix, plain, enriched	15.9	109.8	303.0	31	2+0+5	38-48
corn						
field, whole-grain, raw	40.4	17.7	327.5	31	3+3+0	37-46
sweet						
canned						
cream style	9.5	2.7	90.7	8	2+5+5	20-25
vacuum pack, yellow	11.3	2.3	93.0	9	2+5+5	21-26
wet pack, white and yellow	8.6	2.7	71.2	7	2+5+5	19-24
frozen, kernels cut off cob	14.1	2.3	89.4	9	3+5+3	20-25
raw, on cob	5.7	1.6	36.1	4	2+5+0	11-14
corn flour	35.4	11.8	348.4	30	1+0+0	31-39
corn grits, degermed, enriched	39.5	3.6	354.3	31	5+1+1	38-48
corn products used mainly as ready-to-eat breakfast cereals						
corn flakes						
added nutrients	35.8	1.8	386.9	31	3+1+10	45-56
added nutrients, sugar covered	20.0	.9	414.1	26	3+1+10	40-50
corn, puffed						
added nutrients	36.7	19.1	366.5	32	3+1+10	46-58
presweetened						
added nutrients	18.1	.9	407.3	25	3+1+10	39-49
cocoa-flavored	28.1	10.0	393.3	29	3+1+10	43-54
fruit-flavored	25.4	12.2	396.4	28	3+1+10	42-53
corn, shredded, added nutrients	31.8	1.8	394.2	30	3+1+10	44-55
corn, rice, wheat flakes, mixed	33.6	3.2	390.5	30	3+1+10	44-55

Food						
cornbread mix	34.0	58.1	322.1	33	3+1+0+3	40-50
cornmeal, white or yellow						
bolted (nearly whole-grain)	40.8	15.4	337.9	32	3+1+0+0	36-45
whole ground	41.7	17.7	334.3	32	3+1+0+0	36-45
cornstarch	1.4	0	397.4	19	0+0+0+0	19-24
cowpeas, including blackeye peas						
immature seeds, raw, shelled	40.8	3.6	98.9	19	3+2+0+0	24-30
mature, dry	103.4	6.8	279.9	50	3+2+0+2	57-71
crab						
canned	78.9	11.3	5.0	57	5+0+0+10	72-90
cooked, meat only	78.5	8.6	2.3	57	5+0+0+5	67-84
crackers						
animal	29.9	42.6	362.4	32	2+1+0+10	45-56
cheese	50.8	96.6	274.0	40	2+0+0+10	52-65
graham, plain	36.3	42.6	332.5	32	2+0+0+10	44-55
saltines	40.8	54.4	324.3	35	2+0+0+10	47-59
sandwich type, peanut-cheese	68.9	108.4	254.5	47	2+0+0+10	59-74
soda	41.7	59.4	320.2	35	2+0+0+10	47-59
whole wheat	38.1	62.6	309.4	34	2+1+0+10	47-59
cranberries						
canned sauce, sweetened	.5	.9	170.1	8	0+0+0+5	13-16
cocktail juice, bottled	.5	.5	74.8	4	0+0+0+2	6-8
raw	1.7	3.0	47.0	3	1+3+0+0	7-9
crappie, white, raw, flesh only	76.2	3.6	0	54	5+0+0+3	62-78
cream, fluid						
half-and-half	14.5	53.1	20.9	16	3+0+0+0	19-24
heavy, whipping	10.0	170.6	14.1	12	3+0+0+0	15-19
light, coffee or table	13.6	93.4	19.5	15	3+0+0+0	18-23
light, whipping	11.3	142.0	16.3	13	3+0+0+0	16-20

41

1 Food	2 Protein gm/lb.	3 Fat gm/lb.	4 Carbo-hydrate gm/lb.	5 Value of major nutrients per pound	6 Increments for vitamins, rough-age, seasoning effect and preparation	7 Fair value range per pound as purchased
cream substitutes, dried, containing						
cream, skim milk, lactose	38.6	121.1	278.1	52	3+0+0+3	58-73
cream, skim milk, lactose, sodium hexametaphosphate	63.1	125.6	241.3	68	3+0+0+3	74-93
cucumbers, raw, whole	3.9	.4	14.7	2	3+5+2+0	12-15
currants, raw						
black, European	7.6	.4	58.2	5	5+5+3+0	18-23
red and white	6.2	.9	53.2	5	3+5+3+0	16-20
dandelion greens, raw, trimmed	12.2	3.2	41.7	7	10+5+3+0	25-31
dates						
with pits	8.7	2.0	287.7	17	3+5+2+0	27-34
without pits	10.0	2.3	330.7	19	3+5+2+1	30-38
doughnuts						
cake type	20.9	84.4	233.2	27	3+5+0+10	45-56
yeast-leavened	28.6	121.1	171.0	30	3+5+0+10	48-60
duck, domesticated, ready-to-cook	59.5	106.4	0	47	4+0+0+0	51-64
eggbeater (frozen)	50.0	57.0	0	41	6+0+5+10	62-78
eggright (dry)	252.0	54.0	99.0	188	5+0+2+10	205-256
eggs, chicken						
dried, whole	221.8	194.6	11.3	162	5+0+5+5	177-221
raw, whole, fresh	52.1	46.4	3.6	42	5+0+1+0	48-60
eggplant, raw	4.4	.7	20.6	3	2+5+2+0	12-15
endive, raw, good quality	6.8	.4	16.4	3	5+5+0+0	13-16

Food						
farina, enriched						
instant cooking	51.7	4.1	339.7	34	5+0+0+2	41-51
regular cooking	51.7	4.1	349.3	35	5+0+0+0	40-50
fats, cooking (vegetable)	0	454.0	0	45	0+0+0+0	45-56
figs						
canned, extra heavy sirup	2.3	.9	121.1	6	1+5+0+5	17-21
dried	19.5	5.9	313.4	22	1+5+0+5	33-58
raw	5.4	1.4	92.1	6	1+5+0+0	12-15
filberts, shelled	57.2	283.0	75.8	52	3+2+0+3	60-75
finnan haddie (smoked haddock)						
flesh only, raw	105.2	1.8	0	75	1+0+0+0	76-95
flatfishes (flounders, soles and sanddabs), raw						
flesh only	75.8	3.6	0	54	5+0+0+3	62-78
whole	25.0	1.2	0	18	5+0+0+0	23-29
fruit cocktail, canned						
heavy sirup	1.8	.5	89.4	5	1+5+0+5	16-20
water pack	1.8	.5	44.0	3	1+5+0+5	14-18
gelatin desserts, plain	6.8	0	64.0	8	0+0+0+5	13-16
grapefruit						
juice, canned						
sweetened	2.3	.5	58.1	4	5+0+0+5	14-18
unsweetened	2.3	.5	44.5	3	5+0+0+5	13-16
raw, all varieties	2.3	.5	41.7	3	5+2+0+0	10-13
grapefruit and orange juice, blended						
canned						
sweetened	2.3	.5	55.3	3	5+0+0+5	13-16
unsweetened	2.7	.9	45.8	3	5+0+0+5	13-16
frozen concentrate, unsweetened	9.5	2.3	168.3	11	5+0+0+8	24-30

Food	Protein gm/lb.	Fat gm/lb.	Carbohydrate gm/lb.	Value of major nutrients per pound	Increments for vitamins, roughage, seasoning effect and preparation	Fair value range per pound as purchased
grapes, raw	3.7	2.9	44.9	4	1+5+0+0	10-13
grape juice						
canned or bottled	.9	0	75.3	4	1+0+0+5	10-13
frozen concentrate, sweetened	2.7	.1	210.0	11	2+0+0+8	21-26
haddock						
raw						
flesh only	83.0	.5	0	59	5+0+0+3	67-84
whole	39.8	.2	0	28	5+0+0+0	33-41
smoked	105.2	1.8	0	75	3+0+0+5	83-104
halibut, Atlantic & Pacific, raw						
flesh only	94.8	5.4	0	68	5+0+0+3	76-95
whole	55.9	3.2	0	40	5+0+0+0	45-56
halibut, smoked	94.3	68.0	0	74	0+0+0+3	77-96
heart, beef, lean, raw	77.6	16.3	3.2	57	5+0+0+0	62-78
herring						
Atlantic, raw						
flesh only	78.5	51.3	0	61	5+0+0+3	69-86
whole	40.0	26.1	0	31	5+0+0+0	36-45
canned						
in tomato sauce	71.7	47.6	16.8	56	3+0+0+5	64-80
plain	90.3	61.7	0	70	3+0+0+5	78-98
Pacific, flesh only, raw	79.4	11.8	0	57	5+0+0+3	65-81
pickled, Bismarck type	92.5	68.5	0	72	0+0+0+5	77-96
salted or brined	86.2	68.9	0	68	0+0+0+1	69-86
smoked						
bloaters	88.9	56.2	0	69	0+0+0+2	71-89
kippered	100.7	58.5	0	77	0+0+0+3	80-100

Food					
honey, strained or extracted	1.4	0	373.3	18	0+0+0+5	23-29
horseradish, prepared	5.9	.9	43.5	6	0+5+5+0	16-20
ice cream and frozen custard						
regular						
approximately 10% fat	20.4	48.1	94.3	23	4+0+0+0	27-34
approximately 12% fat	18.1	56.7	93.4	22	4+0+0+0	26-33
rich, approximately 16% fat	11.8	73.0	81.6	17	4+0+0+0	21-26
ice milk	21.8	23.1	101.6	22	4+0+0+0	26-33
ices, water, lime	1.8	0	147.9	8	0+0+0+0	8-10
jams and preserves	2.7	.5	317.5	17	0+2+10+5	34-43
jellies	.5	.5	320.2	15	0+0+10+5	30-38
Jerusalem-artichokes, raw	7.2	.3	52.3	5	2+5+0+0	12-15
kale						
leaves without stems, raw	17.4	2.3	26.1	8	10+5+0+0	23-29
frozen	14.5	2.3	24.9	7	10+5+0+0	22-28
kidneys, beef, raw	69.9	30.4	4.1	53	5+0+0+0	58-73
kohlrabi, stems only, raw	6.6	.3	21.9	3	5+5+0+0	13-16
lake trout, raw						
drawn	30.7	16.8	0	23	5+0+0+0	28-35
fillets	83.0	45.4	0	63	5+0+0+3	71-89
lamb, choice cut						
leg						
with bone	67.7	61.7	0	52	5+0+0+0	57-71
without bone	80.7	73.5	0	62	5+0+0+0	67-84
loin						
with bone	63.7	97.0	0	50	5+0+0+0	55-69
without bone	73.9	112.5	0	57	5+0+0+0	62-78

Food	Protein gm/lb.	Fat gm/lb.	Carbo-hydrate gm/lb.	Value of major nutrients per pound	Increments for vitamins, rough-age, seasoning effect and preparation	Fair value range per pound as purchased
lamb, choice cut (cont.)						
rib						
with bone	54.7	110.2	0	43	5+0+0+0	48-60
without bone	68.5	137.9	0	53	5+0+0+0	58-73
lard	0	454.0	0	5	0+0+0+0	5-6
lemons with peel, raw	5.4	1.3	48.1	4	4+0+4+0	12-15
lemon juice						
canned or bottled, unsweetened	1.8	.5	34.5	2	4+0+4+5	15-19
frozen						
single-strength	1.8	.9	32.7	2	4+0+4+5	15-19
concentrate	10.4	4.1	169.6	12	5+0+6+5	28-35
lemonade concentrate, frozen	.9	.5	231.8	11	5+0+0+5	21-26
lentils, mature seeds, dry, raw, whole	112.0	5.0	272.6	53	2+2+0+1	58-73
lettuce, crisphead varieties good quality, raw	3.9	.4	12.5	2	2+5+0+0	9-11
liver, raw						
beef	90.3	17.2	24.0	67	12+0+0+0	79-99
calf	87.1	21.3	18.6	65	12+0+0+0	77-96
chicken, all classes	89.4	16.8	13.2	66	12+0+0+0	78-98
hog	93.4	16.8	11.8	68	12+0+0+0	80-100
lamb	95.3	17.7	13.2	70	12+0+0+0	82-103
turkey, all classes	96.2	18.1	13.2	71	10+0+0+0	81-101
lobster, northern, raw						
meat only	76.9	8.6	2.3	55	2+0+0+0	57-71
whole	19.9	2.2	.6	14	1+0+0+0	15-19

macaroni						
enriched	56.7	5.4	341.1	36	5+0+0+5	46-58
unenriched	56.7	5.4	341.1	36	0+0+0+5	41-51
macaroni and cheese, canned	17.7	18.1	48.5	10	1+0+0+5	16-20
mackerel						
Atlantic						
canned	87.5	50.3	0	67	2+0+0+5	80-100
whole, raw	46.5	29.9	0	36	5+0+0+0	41-51
Pacific						
canned	95.7	45.4	0	72	3+0+0+5	80-100
dressed	71.5	23.8	0	53	5+0+0+2	60-75
flesh only	99.3	33.1	0	74	5+0+0+3	82-103
mangos, raw	2.1	1.2	51.1	3	5+5+0+0	13-16
margarine	2.7	367.0	1.8	39	5+0+3+0	47-59
marmalade, citrus	2.3	.5	318.0	15	0+3+3+5	26-33
milk, cow						
fluid (pasteurized and raw)						
whole, 3.5% fat	15.9	15.9	22.2	8	2+0+0+4	14-18
skim	16.3	.5	23.1	7	2+0+0+5	14-18
canned						
condensed (sweetened)	36.7	39.5	246.3	28	3+0+0+5	36-45
evaporated (unsweetened)	31.8	35.8	44.0	17	3+0+0+5	25-31
dry						
skim						
instant	162.4	3.2	234.1	69	3+0+0+5	77-96
regular	162.8	3.6	237.2	69	3+0+0+5	77-96
whole	119.8	124.7	173.3	63	5+0+0+5	73-91
malted						
beverage	21.3	20.0	53.1	12	2+0+0+3	17-21
dry powder	66.7	37.6	321.1	42	5+0+0+5	52-65
chocolate drink, fluid, commercial						
made with skim milk	15.0	10.4	49.4	9	2+0+0+3	14-18
made with whole milk	15.4	15.4	49.9	9	2+0+0+3	14-18

	2	3	4	5	6	7
1						
Food	Protein gm/lb.	Fat gm/lb.	Carbo-hydrate gm/lb.	Value of major nutrients per pound	Increments for vitamins, rough-age, seasoning effect and preparation	Fair value range per pound as purchased
millet, whole grain	44.9	13.2	330.7	32	5+0+0+0	37-46
molasses, cane						
first extraction, or light	0	0	295.0	14	0+0+5+0	19-24
second extraction, or medium	0	0	272.0	13	0+0+5+0	18-23
third extraction, or blackstrap	0	0	249.0	11	0+0+5+0	16-20
muffin mix with enriched flour	28.1	52.2	325.7	30	5+0+0+2	37-46
muffins, baked from home-type recipe						
corn, made with enriched cornmeal	32.2	45.8	218.2	26	5+0+0+10	41-51
plain, made with enriched flour	35.4	45.8	191.9	26	5+0+0+10	41-51
mushrooms, raw, good quality	11.9	1.3	19.4	5	5+5+4+0	19-24
muskmelons, raw						
cantaloups	1.6	.2	17.0	1	5+5+0+0	11-14
casaba	2.7	0	14.7	2	2+5+0+0	9-11
honeydew	2.3	.9	22.0	2	2+5+0+0	9-11
mussels, Atlantic & Pacific, raw meat and liquid in shell	22.2	3.2	7.2	16	3+0+0+0	19-24
mustard greens, raw	9.5	1.6	17.8	4	10+5+0+0	19-24
nectarines, raw	2.5	0	71.4	4	5+5+0+0	14-18
noodles, chow mein, canned	59.9	106.6	263.1	44	0+0+0+5	49-61

noodles, egg, enriched	58.1	20.9	326.6	38	5+0+0+4	47-59
oat products used mainly as hot breakfast cereals						
oat cereal with wheat germ and soy grits	93.0	40.8	265.8	49	4+1+0+0	54-68
oat flakes, instant cooking	66.2	19.1	328.0	40	1+1+0+2	44-55
oat granules, quick-cooking	67.1	18.1	328.9	41	1+1+0+2	45-56
oat and wheat cereal	66.7	22.7	309.8	40	3+1+0+2	46-58
oatmeal (rolled oats)	64.4	33.6	309.4	40	3+1+0+0	44-55
oat products used mainly as ready-to-eat breakfast cereals						
flaked	67.6	25.9	320.7	41	5+1+0+10	57-71
puffed	54.0	24.9	341.1	37	3+1+0+10	51-64
puffed, sugar coated	30.4	15.4	388.3	30	3+1+0+10	44-55
shredded	85.3	9.5	326.6	46	10+1+0+10	67-84
oils, salad or cooking	0	454.0	0	45	0+0+0+0	45-56
okra						
frozen, cuts and pods	10.4	.5	40.8	6	5+5+0+0	16-20
raw, good quality	9.4	1.2	29.6	5	5+5+0+0	15-19
olives, pickled, canned, or bottled						
green						
with pits	3.4	30.5	3.1	4	1+5+0+3	13-16
without pits	3.4	30.5	3.1	4	1+5+0+3	13-16
ripe (ascolano)						
with pits	2.2	28.2	5.3	4	0+5+0+3	12-15
without pits	2.3	29.4	5.5	4	0+5+0+3	12-15
ripe, salt cured, oil-coated	8.0	129.9	31.6	17	0+5+0+3	25-31
onions						
mature, dry						
dehydrated, flaked	39.5	5.9	372.4	32	5+5+15+5	62-78
raw	6.2	.4	35.9	4	3+5+5+0	17-21
young, green, raw	1.8	.3	17.6	1	3+5+5+0	14-18
Welsh, raw	5.6	1.2	19.2	3	3+5+5+0	16-20

1	2	3	4	5	6	7
Food	Protein gm/lb.	Fat gm/lb.	Carbo-hydrate gm/lb.	Value of major nutrients per pound	Increments for vitamins, rough-age, seasoning effect and preparation	Fair value range per pound as purchased
orange juice						
canned						
sweetened	3.2	.9	55.3	4	5+0+1+5	15-19
unsweetened	3.6	.9	50.8	4	5+0+1+5	15-19
unsweetened concentrate	18.6	5.9	230.0	18	10+0+2+5	35-44
dehydrated	22.7	7.7	403.3	27	15+0+4+7	53-66
frozen, concentrate, unsweetened	10.4	.9	172.4	12	10+0+2+5	29-36
oranges, raw						
used for fruit	3.3	.7	40.4	3	5+5+1+0	14-18
used for juice	3.2	.9	47.2	3	5+5+1+0	14-18
orange and apricot juice drink, canned	1.4	.5	57.6	3	5+0+0+5	13-16
oyster stew, frozen, condensed	20.9	28.6	31.3	19	2+0+0+5	26-33
oysters, eastern, raw						
in shell	3.8	.8	1.5	3	1+0+0+0	4-5
meat only	38.1	8.2	15.4	29	5+0+0+1	35-44
pancake and waffle mixes						
buckwheat and other cereal flours	47.6	8.6	318.9	32	5+0+0+3	40-50
plain and buttermilk with enriched flour	39.0	8.2	343.4	30	5+0+0+3	38-48
parsnips, raw	6.6	1.9	67.5	6	3+5+0+0	14-18
pastinas, enriched, egg	58.5	18.6	325.7	38	5+0+0+3	46-58
pate de foie gras, canned	51.7	198.7	21.8	42	5+0+0+5	52-65

peach nectar, canned	.9	.2	56.2	3	2+0+0+5	10-13
peaches						
canned						
heavy sirup	1.8	.5	91.2	5	4+5+0+5	19-24
juice pack	2.7	.5	52.6	3	4+5+0+5	17-21
dehydrated	21.8	4.1	399.2	27	5+5+0+5	42-53
dried, sulfured	14.1	3.2	309.8	20	5+5+0+5	35-44
frozen, sliced, sweetened	1.8	.5	102.5	5	4+5+0+3	17-21
raw, peeled fruit	2.4	.4	38.3	3	4+5+0+0	12-15
peanut butter made with						
small amount of added fat and salt	126.1	224.1	78.0	71	8+0+0+0	79-99
small amount of added fat, sweetener, and salt	115.7	224.5	88.5	68	8+0+0+0	76-95
moderate amount of added fat, sweetener, and salt	114.3	229.5	85.3	67	8+0+0+0	75-94
peanut spread	92.1	236.3	99.8	61	7+0+0+0	68-85
peanuts, roasted						
in shell	79.6	148.0	62.6	46	8+0+0+1	55-69
shelled	118.8	220.9	93.4	69	10+0+0+2	81-101
pear nectar, canned	1.4	.9	59.9	3	1+0+0+5	9-11
pears						
canned						
heavy sirup	.9	.9	88.9	4	1+5+0+5	15-19
juice pack	1.4	1.4	53.5	3	1+5+0+5	14-18
water pack	.9	.9	37.6	2	1+5+0+5	13-16
dried, sulfured	14.1	8.2	305.3	20	1+5+0+5	31-39
raw for fruit	2.9	1.7	63.2	4	1+5+0+0	10-13
peas, green, immature						
canned, regular pack						
Alaska (early or June)	15.9	1.4	56.7	8	3+3+0+5	19-24
sweet	15.4	1.4	47.2	8	3+3+0+5	19-24

Food	Protein gm/lb.	Fat gm/lb.	Carbohydrate gm/lb.	Value of major nutrients per pound	Increments for vitamins, roughage, seasoning effect and preparation	Fair value range per pound as purchased
peas, green, immature (cont.)						
frozen	24.5	1.4	58.1	11	5+5+0+3	24-30
raw						
in pod	10.9	.7	24.8	5	2+3+0+0	10-13
shelled	28.6	1.8	65.3	13	5+5+0+3	26-33
peas, mature seeds, dry, raw						
split, without seed coat	109.8	4.5	284.4	52	4+5+0+5	66-83
whole	109.3	5.9	273.5	52	4+5+0+5	66-83
peas and carrots, frozen	15.0	1.4	47.2	8	10+5+0+3	26-33
pecans						
in shell	22.1	171.2	35.1	27	1+0+0+0	28-35
shelled	41.7	323.0	66.2	50	2+0+0+3	55-69
peppers, hot, chili immature, green						
canned						
chili sauce	3.2	.5	22.7	2	10+5+3+5	25-31
pods, excluding seeds	4.1	.5	27.7	3	10+5+3+5	26-33
raw	4.3	.7	30.1	3	10+5+3+0	21-26
mature, red						
canned, chili sauce	4.1	2.7	17.7	3	10+3+10+5	31-39
dried						
chili powder	64.9	56.2	256.3	40	25+5+10+3	83-104
pods	58.5	41.3	271.3	37	30+5+10+3	85-106
raw						
pods, excluding seeds	7.6	1.3	52.3	5	15+5+5+0	30-38
pods, including seeds	16.1	10.0	78.8	10	20+5+5+0	40-50
peppers, sweet garden variety						
green, raw	4.5	.7	17.9	2	5+5+10+0	22-28
red, raw	5.1	1.1	25.8	3	10+5+10+0	28-35

perch, raw						
yellow						
flesh only	88.5	4.1	0	63	5+0+0+3	71-89
whole	34.5	1.6	0	25	5+0+0+0	30-38
white						
flesh only	87.5	18.1	0	64	5+0+0+3	72-90
whole	31.5	6.5	0	23	5+0+0+0	28-35
persimmons, raw						
Japanese or kaki varieties						
with seeds	2.6	1.5	73.3	4	5+5+0+0	14-18
without seeds	2.7	1.5	75.1	5	5+5+0+0	15-19
native	3.0	1.5	124.6	7	5+5+0+0	17-21
pickles						
cucumber						
dill	3.2	.9	10.0	2	1+5+0+3	11-14
fresh (as bread-and-butter pickles)	4.1	.9	81.2	5	1+5+0+3	14-18
sour	2.3	.9	9.1	1	1+5+0+3	10-13
sweet	3.2	1.8	165.6	9	1+5+0+3	18-23
chowchow						
sour	6.4	5.9	18.6	4	1+5+0+5	15-19
sweet	6.8	4.1	122.5	8	1+5+0+5	19-24
relish						
sour	3.2	4.1	12.2	2	1+5+0+5	13-16
sweet	2.3	2.7	154.2	8	1+5+0+5	19-24
pies						
baked, piecrust made with enriched flour						
apple	10.0	50.3	172.8	17	1+2+0+10	30-38
cherry	11.8	51.3	174.2	17	1+2+0+10	30-38
chocolate chiffon	30.8	69.4	198.2	27	2+0+0+10	39-49
custard	27.7	50.3	106.1	20	1+0+0+10	31-39
lemon chiffon	31.8	57.2	198.7	26	1+0+0+10	37-46
lemon meringue	16.8	46.3	171.0	18	1+0+0+10	29-36
mince	11.3	52.2	186.9	18	1+1+0+10	30-38
peach	11.3	48.5	173.3	17	3+2+0+10	32-40

Food	Protein gm/lb.	Fat gm/lb.	Carbo-hydrate gm/lb.	Value of major nutrients per pound	Increments for vitamins, rough-age, seasoning effect and preparation	Fair value range per pound as purchased
1	2	3	4	5	6	7
pies (cont.)						
baked, piecrust made with enriched flour (cont.)						
pecan	23.1	103.9	232.7	29	1+0+0+10	40-50
pineapple	10.0	48.5	172.8	16	1+2+0+10	29-36
pineapple chiffon	29.9	54.9	177.4	24	1+2+0+10	37-46
pumpkin	18.1	50.8	111.1	17	4+3+0+10	34-43
strawberry	8.6	35.8	140.2	13	4+4+0+10	31-39
frozen in unbaked form						
apple	7.3	37.6	150.6	13	1+2+0+5	21-26
cherry	8.6	48.1	176.9	16	3+2+0+10	31-39
coconut custard	23.6	38.6	122.9	18	1+1+0+10	30-38
piecrust mix, including stick form	32.7	148.3	224.5	37	0+0+0+5	42-53
pimentos, canned	4.1	2.3	26.3	3	8+5+0+5	21-26
pineapple						
canned						
heavy sirup	1.4	.5	88.0	5	3+5+2+5	20-25
juice pack	1.8	.5	68.5	4	3+5+2+5	19-24
water pack	1.4	.5	46.3	3	3+5+0+5	16-20
raw	.9	.5	32.3	2	3+5+0+0	10-13
pineapple juice						
canned, unsweetened	1.8	.5	61.2	4	3+0+0+5	12-15
frozen concentrate, unsweetened	5.9	.5	200.9	11	5+0+0+5	21-26
pineapple and grapefruit juice drink, canned	.9	0	61.7	3	3+0+0+5	11-14

Food					
pizza, with cheese					
from home-type recipe, baked					
with cheese topping	54.4	37.6	128.4	29	4+0+0+10	43-54
with sausage topping	35.4	42.2	134.3	23	4+0+0+10	37-46
frozen, partially baked	40.4	29.9	150.1	24	4+0+0+5	33-41
plate dinners, frozen, commercial					
beef pot roast, whole oven-					
browned potatoes, peas,					
and corn	59.4	14.5	27.7	45	3+2+0+10	60-75
chicken, fried; mashed					
potatoes, mixed vegetables	54.5	36.2	48.1	45	3+2+0+10	60-75
meat loaf with tomato sauce,					
mashed potatoes, and peas	36.3	30.4	44.5	31	3+2+0+10	46-58
turkey, sliced; mashed pota-					
toes, and peas	38.1	13.6	57.6	31	3+2+0+10	46-58
plums					
canned					
greengage	1.7	.4	37.5	2	2+5+0+5	14-18
purple (Italian prunes)					
heavy sirup	1.7	.4	94.1	5	2+5+0+5	17-21
water pack	1.7	.9	51.8	3	2+5+0+5	15-19
raw					
damson	2.1	0	73.5	4	2+5+0+0	11-14
prune-type	3.4	.9	84.0	5	2+5+0+0	12-15
pollock, raw					
drawn	41.6	1.8	0	30	5+0+0+0	35-44
fillets	92.5	4.1	0	66	5+0+0+3	74-93
pompano, raw					
flesh only	85.3	43.1	0	65	5+0+0+3	73-91
whole	47.8	24.1	0	36	5+0+0+0	41-51
popcorn, unpopped	54.0	21.3	327.0	36	2+0+0+0	38-48
pork, fresh, medium-fat, raw					
bacon or belly					
without skin	37.2	278.1	0	31	3+0+0+0	34-43

Food	Protein gm/lb.	Fat gm/lb.	Carbohydrate gm/lb.	Value of major nutrients per pound	Increments for vitamins, roughage, seasoning effect and preparation	Fair value range per pound as purchased
1	2	3	4	5	6	7
pork, fresh, medium-fat, raw (cont.)						
Boston butt						
with bone and skin	65.9	104.1	0	51	4+0+0	55-69
without bone and skin	70.3	111.1	0	54	4+0+0	58-73
ham						
with bone and skin	61.3	102.6	0	48	4+0+0	52-65
without bone and skin	72.1	120.7	0	56	4+0+0	60-75
loin						
with bone	61.1	89.0	0	48	4+0+0	52-65
without bone	77.6	112.9	0	60	4+0+0	64-80
picnic						
with bone and skin	59.0	92.2	0	46	4+0+0	50-63
without bone and skin	71.7	112.0	0	55	4+0+0	59-74
shoulder						
without bone and skin	57.6	174.6	0	45	4+0+0	49-61
spareribs						
with bone	39.2	89.7	0	32	4+0+0	36-45
without bone	65.8	150.6	0	51	4+0+0	55-69
pork, cured, canned						
ham	83.0	55.8	4.1	64	5+0+5	74-93
pork, long-cure, dry ham, medium-fat						
with bone and skin	66.7	138.0	1.2	52	4+0+4	60-75
without bone and skin	76.7	159.0	1.4	59	4+0+4	67-84
pork and gravy, canned (90% pork, 10% gravy)	74.0	80.7	28.6	59	4+0+5	68-85
potato chips	24.0	180.5	226.8	37	5+5+5	52-65
potato flour	36.3	3.6	362.4	30	4+0+0	34-43

potatoes						
canned, solids and liquid	5.0	.9	44.5	4	2+4+0+5	15-19
dehydrated, mashed						
flakes without milk	32.7	2.7	381.0	29	5+5+0+5	44-55
granules with milk	49.4	5.0	352.4	34	5+5+0+5	49-61
granules without milk	37.6	2.7	364.7	30	5+5+0+5	45-56
frozen						
french fried	12.7	29.5	118.4	13	4+5+0+5	27-34
mashed	7.7	.5	77.6	6	4+5+0+3	18-23
raw	7.7	.4	62.8	6	3+5+0+0	14-18
pretzels	44.5	20.4	344.3	34	0+0+0+10	44-55
prune juice, canned or bottled	1.8	.5	86.2	5	2+0+0+5	12-15
prunes, dried, large	8.4	2.4	269.1	16	3+5+1+5	30-38
pudding mix with starch base						
chocolate, regular	13.6	9.5	415.0	25	0+0+0+3	28-35
pumpkin						
canned	4.5	1.4	35.8	3	5+5+3+5	21-26
raw	3.2	.3	20.6	2	3+5+3+0	13-16
radishes, raw, without tops	4.1	.4	14.7	2	3+5+0+0	10-13
raisins, natural	11.3	.9	351.1	20	0+5+5+5	35-44
raspberries, red						
canned	3.2	.5	39.9	3	3+5+0+5	16-20
frozen, sweetened	3.2	.9	111.6	6	3+5+0+3	17-21
raw	5.3	2.2	59.8	5	3+5+0+5	13-16
rhubarb						
frozen, sweetened	2.7	.9	83.9	5	2+5+0+1	13-16
raw, without leaves	2.3	.4	14.4	2	2+5+0+0	9-11
rice						
brown, raw	34.0	8.6	351.1	29	5+0+0+0	34-43

Food	Protein gm/lb.	Fat gm/lb.	Carbohydrate gm/lb.	Value of major nutrients per pound	Increments for vitamins, roughage, seasoning effect and preparation	Fair value range per pound as purchased
rice (cont.)						
white						
common varieties,						
enriched, raw	30.4	1.8	364.7	28	4+0+0+0	32-40
long-grain, parboiled	33.6	1.4	368.8	29	4+0+0+0	33-41
rice products used mainly as hot breakfast cereals						
rice, granulated, added nutrients	27.2	1.4	389.6	28	5+0+0+0	33-41
rice products used mainly as ready-to-eat breakfast cereals, with added nutrients						
rice flakes	26.8	1.4	397.8	28	5+0+0+10	43-54
rice, puffed or oven-popped, presweetened						
honey	19.1	3.2	411.0	26	5+0+0+10	41-51
honey or cocoa plus fat	20.4	18.1	393.3	27	5+0+0+10	42-53
rice, shredded	23.6	1.4	402.8	27	5+0+0+10	42-53
rice with protein concentrate, mainly						
casein	181.4	.9	248.6	76	10+0+0+10	96-120
wheat gluten	90.7	1.4	337.5	48	8+0+0+10	66-83
rolls and buns						
ready-to-serve						
Danish pastry	33.6	106.6	206.8	32	2+0+0+10	44-55
hard, enriched flour	44.5	14.5	269.9	30	5+0+0+10	45-56
plain, enriched flour	37.2	25.4	240.4	27	5+0+0+10	42-53
sweet	38.6	41.3	223.6	28	2+0+0+10	40-50
whole wheat	45.4	12.7	237.2	28	5+0+0+10	43-54

partially baked (brown and serve) enriched flour	35.8	30.8	229.5	26	5+0+0+5	36-45
roll dough, frozen enriched flour	34.0	22.7	215.0	24	5+0+0+3	32-40
rutabagas, without tops	4.2	.4	42.4	3	5+5+0+0	13-16
rye flours dark	73.9	11.8	308.9	42	5+0+0+0	47-59
light	42.6	4.5	353.4	32	1+0+0+0	33-41
medium	51.7	7.7	339.3	35	5+0+0+0	40-50
whole grain	54.9	7.7	332.9	36	3+0+0+0	39-49
rye wafers, whole grain	59.0	5.4	346.1	37	3+0+0+10	50-63
salad dressings, commercial blue and roquefort cheese, regular	21.8	237.2	33.6	41	0+0+0+5	46-58
French, regular	2.7	176.5	79.4	23	0+0+0+5	28-35
Italian, regular	.9	272.2	31.3	29	0+0+0+5	34-43
mayonnaise	5.0	362.4	10.0	40	0+0+0+5	45-56
Russian	7.3	230.4	47.2	30	0+0+0+5	35-44
thousand island, regular	3.6	227.7	69.9	29	0+0+0+5	34-43
salmon Atlantic canned, solids and liquid	98.4	55.3	0	75	0+0+0+5	80-100
raw flesh only	102.1	60.8	0	78	5+0+0+2	85-106
whole	66.3	39.5	0	51	5+0+0+0	56-70
smoked	98.0	42.2	0	74	0+0+0+3	77-96
sockeye (red), canned	92.1	42.2	0	70	5+0+0+5	80-100
sandwich spread with chopped pickle, regular	3.2	164.2	72.1	22	0+2+3+3	30-38

Food	Protein gm/lb.	Fat gm/lb.	Carbohydrate gm/lb.	Value of major nutrients per pound	Increments for vitamins, roughage, seasoning effect and preparation	Fair value range per pound as purchased
1	2	3	4	5	6	7
sardines						
Atlantic, canned in oil	93.4	110.7	2.7	77	3+0+5	85-106
Pacific, canned						
in brine or mustard	85.3	54.4	7.7	66	0+0+5	71-89
in tomato sauce	84.8	55.3	7.7	66	3+0+5	74-93
sauerkraut, canned	4.5	.9	18.1	3	3+5+5	16-20
sausage, cold cuts, and luncheon meats						
bologna						
all samples	54.9	124.7	5.0	44	2+0+3	49-61
all meat	60.3	103.4	16.8	48	2+0+3	53-66
country-style sausage	68.5	141.1	0	53	2+0+0	55-69
deviled ham, canned	63.1	146.5	0	49	2+0+5	56-70
frankfurters						
all samples, raw	56.7	125.2	8.2	45	2+0+0	47-59
canned	60.8	82.1	.9	48	2+0+5	55-69
liverwurst						
fresh	73.5	116.1	8.2	57	5+0+0	62-78
smoked	67.1	124.3	10.4	53	5+0+1	59-74
luncheon meat						
boiled ham	86.2	77.1	0	66	4+0+5	75-94
pork, cured ham or shoulder, spiced, or unspiced, canned	68.0	112.9	5.9	53	4+0+5	62-78
meat loaf	72.1	59.9	15.0	56	4+0+5	65-81
meat, potted (includes beef, chicken, and turkey)	79.4	87.1	0	61	2+0+5	68-85
salami, dry	108.0	172.8	5.4	81	4+0+3	88-110
scrapple	39.9	61.7	66.2	36	3+0+0	39-49
Vienna sausage, canned	63.5	89.8	1.4	50	3+0+5	58-73

scallops, bay and sea, raw	69.4	.9	15.0	50	4+0+0+0	54-68
shad or American shad						
canned	76.7	39.9	0	58	1+0+0+5	64-80
raw, flesh only	84.4	45.4	0	64	5+0+0+3	72-90
sherbet, orange	4.1	5.4	139.7	10	0+0+0+0	10-13
shrimp						
canned, solids and liquid	73.5	3.6	3.6	53	2+0+0+5	60-75
raw						
in shell	56.7	2.5	4.7	41	5+0+0+0	46-58
flesh only	82.1	3.6	6.8	59	5+0+0+3	67-84
sirup						
cane	0	0	308.0	14	0+0+3+3	20-25
maple	0	0	295.0	14	0+0+3+3	20-25
sorghum	0	0	308.0	14	0+0+3+3	20-25
table blends						
chiefly corn	0	0	340.0	16	0+0+3+3	22-28
chiefly cane and maple	0	0	295.0	14	0+0+3+3	20-25
smelt, Atlantic, raw, whole	46.4	5.2	0	33	5+0+0+0	38-48
soups, commercial						
canned						
asparagus, cream of	9.1	6.4	38.1	9	2+0+0+5	16-20
bean with pork	29.0	20.9	78.5	26	2+0+0+5	33-41
beef broth	19.1	0	10.0	14	2+0+0+5	21-26
beef noodle	14.5	10.0	26.3	12	2+0+0+5	19-24
celery, cream of	6.4	19.1	33.6	8	2+1+0+5	16-20
chicken consomme	12.7	.5	6.8	9	2+0+0+5	16-20
chicken, cream of	10.9	21.8	30.4	11	2+0+0+5	18-23
chicken gumbo	11.8	5.9	27.7	10	2+0+0+5	17-21
chicken noodle	12.7	7.3	29.9	11	2+0+0+5	18-23
chicken with rice	11.8	4.5	21.3	10	2+0+0+5	17-21
chicken vegetable	15.4	9.1	34.9	13	2+2+0+5	22-28
clam chowder, manhattan	8.2	9.5	45.4	9	2+1+0+5	17-21
minestrone	18.1	12.7	52.6	17	2+1+0+5	25-31

Food	Protein gm/lb.	Fat gm/lb.	Carbo-hydrate gm/lb.	Value of major nutrients per pound	Increments for vitamins, rough-age, seasoning effect and preparation	Fair value range per pound as purchased
	2	3	4	5	6	7
1						
soups, commercial (cont.)						
canned (cont.)						
mushroom, cream of	8.6	36.3	38.1	11	2+0+5+5	23-29
onion	20.0	9.5	19.5	16	2+0+5+5	28-35
pea, green	20.9	8.2	83.5	19	2+0+0+5	26-33
pea, split	31.8	11.8	77.1	27	2+0+0+5	34-43
tomato	7.3	9.5	57.6	8	2+0+3+5	18-23
turkey noodle	16.3	10.9	31.8	14	2+0+0+5	21-26
vegetable beef	19.1	8.2	35.8	16	2+3+0+5	26-33
vegetable with beef broth	10.0	6.4	49.9	10	2+0+0+5	17-21
vegetarian vegetable	8.2	7.7	48.1	9	2+4+0+5	20-25
dehydrated mix						
beef noodle	61.7	33.6	296.2	61	5+0+0+5	71-89
chicken noodle	65.8	45.4	263.5	63	5+0+0+5	73-91
chicken rice	40.8	30.8	284.9	45	3+0+0+5	53-66
onion	63.1	48.1	244.5	61	2+0+5+5	73-91
pea, green	101.6	18.6	279.4	87	5+0+0+5	97-121
frozen						
vegetable with beef	24.5	10.4	31.8	20	3+2+0+5	30-38
soybean flour						
full-fat	166.5	92.1	137.9	75	5+0+0+0	80-100
high-fat	186.9	54.9	151.0	79	5+0+0+0	84-105
low-fat	196.9	30.4	166.0	80	5+0+0+0	85-106
soybean protein	339.7	.5	68.5	124	1+0+0+0	125-156
spaghetti, enriched	56.7	5.4	341.1	36	5+0+0+3	44-55
spaghetti in tomato sauce with cheese, canned	10.0	2.7	69.9	7	3+0+0+5	15-19

spaghetti with meat balls in tomato sauce, canned	22.2	18.6	51.7	20	3+0+0+5	28-35
spinach						
canned, regular pack	9.1	1.8	13.6	4	6+5+0+5	20-25
frozen, chopped	14.1	1.4	17.2	6	10+5+0+0	21-26
raw, good quality						
trimmed	14.5	1.4	19.5	6	10+5+0+0	21-26
untrimmed	10.5	1.0	14.0	4	9+5+0+0	18-23
squash						
frozen						
summer	6.4	.5	21.3	3	3+5+0+0	11-14
winter	5.4	1.4	41.7	4	5+5+0+0	14-18
raw, good quality						
summer	4.8	.4	18.5	3	3+5+0+0	11-14
winter	4.5	1.0	39.9	4	5+5+0+0	14-18
strawberries						
frozen, sliced, sweetened	2.3	.9	126.1	8	5+5+0+3	21-26
raw, good quality	3.0	2.2	36.6	3	5+5+0+0	13-16
sturgeon, smoked	141.5	8.2	0	101	0+0+0+3	104-130
succotash, frozen	19.5	1.8	97.5	18	3+5+0+3	29-36
sugars						
beet or cane						
brown	0	0	437.3	20	0+0+3+3	26-33
granulated	0	0	451.3	21	0+0+3+3	27-34
powdered	0	0	451.3	21	0+0+3+3	27-34
maple	0	0	408.0	19	0+0+3+3	25-31
sweet potatoes						
canned, regular pack						
in sirup	4.5	.9	124.7	7	6+5+0+5	23-29
raw	6.2	1.5	96.6	7	10+5+0+0	22-28
tangerines, raw	2.7	.7	38.9	3	5+5+0+0	13-16

Food	Protein gm/lb.	Fat gm/lb.	Carbo-hydrate gm/lb.	Value of major nutrients per pound	Increments for vitamins, rough-age, seasoning effect and preparation	Fair value range per pound as purchased
	2	3	4	5	6	7
tapioca, dry	2.7	.9	391.9	20	0+0+0+3	23-29
tartar sauce, regular	6.4	262.2	19.1	32	0+0+0+3	35-44
tomatoes						
canned, regular pack	4.5	.9	19.5	3	4+5+5+5	22-28
raw, ripe, whole	5.0	.9	21.3	3	5+5+5+0	18-23
tomato catsup, bottled	9.1	1.8	115.2	9	4+0+5+5	23-29
tomato chili sauce, bottled	11.3	1.4	112.5	9	4+0+5+5	23-29
tomato juice						
canned or bottled						
concentrate	15.4	1.8	77.6	9	10+0+0+5	24-30
regular pack	4.1	.5	19.5	2	4+0+0+5	11-14
tomato juice cocktail						
canned or bottled	3.2	.5	22.7	2	4+0+0+5	11-14
tomato paste, canned	15.4	1.8	84.4	10	10+0+10+5	35-44
tomato puree, canned, regular	7.7	.9	40.4	5	5+0+3+5	18-23
trout, rainbow, raw, flesh only	97.5	51.7	0	74	5+0+0+3	82-103
tuna, canned						
in oil	109.8	93.0	0	87	5+0+0+5	97-121
in water	127.0	3.6	0	90	5+0+0+5	100-125
turkey						
canned, meat only	94.8	56.7	0	73	3+0+0+5	81-101

potpie, frozen	26.3	47.2	91.2	28	3+2+0+3	36-45
raw, ready-to-cook	66.6	48.7	0	52	3+0+0+0	55-69
turnips, raw, without tops	3.9	.8	25.7	3	3+5+0+0	11-14
turnip greens						
frozen	11.8	1.4	18.1	5	8+5+0+3	21-26
raw, trimmed	13.6	1.4	22.7	6	10+5+0+0	21-26
veal, medium-fat						
flank						
with bone	74.1	121.0	0	57	5+0+0+0	62-78
without bone	74.8	122.0	0	58	5+0+0+0	63-79
loin						
with bone	72.3	41.0	0	55	5+0+0+0	60-75
without bone	87.1	50.0	0	66	5+0+0+0	71-89
rib						
with bone	65.7	49.0	0	51	5+0+0+0	56-70
without bone	85.3	64.0	0	65	5+0+0+0	70-88
vegetable juice cocktail						
canned	4.1	.5	16.3	2	2+0+0+5	9-11
vegetables, mixed, frozen	15.0	1.4	62.1	8	5+5+0+2	20-25
waffles, frozen, enriched flour	32.2	28.1	190.5	23	3+0+0+5	31-39
waffle mix, enriched flour	29.0	87.1	296.7	33	4+0+0+3	40-50
walnuts						
black, shelled	93.0	269.0	67.1	63	3+3+3+3	75-94
Persian or English in shell	30.2	130.6	32.2	25	3+2+0+0	30-38
shelled	67.1	290.3	71.7	56	5+3+3+3	70-88
watermelon, raw	1.0	.4	13.4	1	2+5+0+0	8-10
wheat bran, crude	72.6	20.9	280.8	41	5+5+0+0	51-64

1	2	3	4	5	6	7
Food	Protein gm/lb.	Fat gm/lb.	Carbo-hydrate gm/lb.	Value of major nutrients per pound	Increments for vitamins, rough-age, seasoning effect and preparation	Fair value range per pound as purchased
wheat flours						
patent						
all-purpose, enriched	47.6	4.5	345.2	33	5+0+0+0	38-48
bread flour, enriched	53.5	5.0	338.8	35	5+0+0+0	40-50
cake, or pastry flour	34.0	3.6	360.2	29	0+0+0+0	29-36
whole	60.3	9.1	322.1	37	5+0+0+0	42-53
wheat germ, crude	120.7	49.4	211.8	57	5+0+0+0	62-78
wheat products used mainly as hot breakfast cereals						
wheat, rolled	44.9	9.1	345.6	33	5+2+0+0	40-50
wheat, whole meal	61.2	9.1	328.0	38	5+2+0+0	45-56
wheat and malted barley, toasted						
instant-cooking	63.5	7.3	345.6	39	1+2+0+0	42-53
quick-cooking	54.4	7.3	356.1	36	1+2+0+0	39-49
wheat products used mainly as ready-to-eat cereals						
wheat flakes	46.3	7.3	365.1	34	5+1+0+10	50-63
wheat germ, toasted	136.1	52.2	224.5	64	5+1+0+10	80-100
wheat puffed	68.0	6.8	356.1	41	5+1+0+10	57-71
wheat, puffed, with honey	27.2	9.5	400.5	29	5+1+0+10	45-56
wheat, shredded	44.9	9.1	362.4	33	5+1+0+10	49-61
wheat, shredded, with malt	41.3	13.2	370.6	33	5+1+0+10	49-61
wheat and malted barley flakes	39.9	5.9	382.4	32	5+1+0+10	48-60
wheat and malted barley granules	45.4	2.7	382.8	34	5+1+0+10	50-63
yam, tuber, raw	8.2	.8	90.5	7	3+5+0+0	15-19

yoghurt					
made with skim milk	15.4	7.7	23.6	13	2+0+0+0	15-19
made with whole milk	13.6	15.4	22.2	12	2+0+0+0	14-18
zwieback	48.5	39.9	337.0	37	3+0+0+10	50-63

Chapter 4

PLANNING A FAMILY MENU

In planning a menu for a family, one must consider not only cost, but nutritional value and acceptability. In general, a reasonable variety of low-cost foods, together with a small amount of the high-priced foods will provide a good nutritional balance.

A key feature in sound planning is a reduction in the amount of meat used, together with the serving of more economical substitutes. Meat is primarily a source of protein. Its carbohydrate content is negligible, and much of its fat content is harmful rather than helpful. Therefore, one must plan on some substitution of lower cost foods to provide the needed protein. The mineral and vitamin content of meats is not critical and can readily be made up by other items in the diet.

The most obvious substitutes for meat are poultry, fish, eggs, and cheese. Unfortunately, these foods are also rising rapidly in price, and if many people try to substitute them for meat completely, their prices will soon come close to those of meat. A *limited* substitution of these foods may be practical, however. The major substitution for meat protein must come from other sources. Fortunately, such sources are readily available in grains, legumes (peas and beans), peanut butter and dried nonfat milk. Although soybeans are a superior substitute for meat, I have omitted soybeans from major consideration because of current evidence that soybean prices are soaring.

A useful plan would be based on purchasing only 1/2 as much meat as before, or in some cases, 2/3 as much meat per week.

Three days of the week meat can be served as before, but in smaller portions. Each portion should be 3/4 of the usual size. If in the past, you bought 2 pounds of beef for a single meal, buy 1 1/2 pounds for a similar meal. To make up the difference in protein, serve an additional dish, or eat more bread with the meal.

Two days of the week, meat-extender dishes or poultry or fish extenders can be served. A meat-extender dish is one which contains meat for flavor and some protein, but also contains a less expensive source of protein to make up the total requirement. In general, a dish of this kind should include no more than two ounces of meat per serving. The most common form of meat-extender dish is meatloaf which contains bread crumbs to increase the total protein at a low cost. Poultry and fish extenders act in a similar way to increase the total protein content at low cost. If the poultry or fish is not overly expensive, one may use up to three ounces per serving.

The other two days of the week, one should avoid meat, poultry, and fish entirely. Instead, protein should be supplied by grains, legumes, peanut butter, nonfat milk, some cheese, and a limited amount of eggs. Planning should also include savings in side dishes, desserts, lunches, breakfasts, and snacks. All these add up, and every penny you save on the food bill is actually a true savings of at least 3 cents.

A certain amount of strategy is helpful in planning a day's menu. If expensive foods such as meat (over 2oz. per person) are served, the other dishes should be economical and should not include meat extenders and protein substitutes as well. If steak, roast beef, or ham is to be served as a main dish, it would be practical to serve potatoes and a cooked vegetable. However, do not serve barley, corn meal or bean dishes, macaroni, spaghetti, cheese, eggs, or nonfat milk. Dessert on a meat day should be simple—perhaps some canned fruit.

If the main dish is to be a meat extender, the rest of the meal can be somewhat more elaborate. If you are not going to have meat, poultry, or fish, go all out in preparing tasty side dishes of high protein value, examples of which are given in the recipe section.

An enriched dessert may also be served, which will lend

additional protein content to the meal and help the family feel more satisfied psychologically. Double desserts, such as pie, cake, or cantaloupe with ice milk, pie with cheese, and pudding with sauce plus fresh fruit, may also help make the non and low-meat meals more popular with a family.

PLANNING FOR ADEQUATE PROTEIN

In planning each meal, it is helpful to concentrate first on the protein content. Protein is ordinarily the most expensive of the major nutrients by a wide margin, and although it is relatively easy to add fats and carbohydrates to a meal, adding protein is a more complex matter. Once the protein components of a meal are determined, it often happens that the fat and carbohydrates are automatically present in proper amounts. Although we will use specific figures concerning protein content, it isn't necessary to remember them, as even a general familiarity with the relative protein contents of foods can help save you money.

Let us start with the protein requirement for adults, and take as a reasonable average *60 grams per day*, or theoretically, 20 grams of protein per person at each meal. Of course, few people eat an ideal diet, and many skimp on breakfast and lunch. Nevertheless, the total savings per day can be figured on the basis of 20 grams of protein per meal. Let us assume, as a useful approximation, that the 20 grams of protein come from two main sources at each meal. By selecting both foods from the cheaper categories, one can save a substantial amount. By choosing one protein source from the cheaper and one from the expensive categories, the savings will be about half as much.* *The table at the end of this chapter is designed to help you determine the market cost of 10 grams of protein in certain selected foods.*

*The cost of proteins in different foods is based on prices in May and June, 1973.

As the price of food varies, the cost of its protein content will vary in direct proportion. For example, if the price of eggs doubles, the cost of the protein in the egg will also double. If the price of ham goes up 25%, add 25% to the cost of the protein in the ham.

The foods in the "Protein-Cost Counter" are "given credit" for their content of fats and carbohydrates, and the value of these components is deducted from the market price. This credit is 1 cent for 10 grams of fat and 0.46 cent for 10 grams of carbohydrate. The reader may be surprised at the high cost of the protein in some common foods. This occurs because protein is present in relatively low concentrations, even in so-called high-protein foods. Keep in mind that the prices given are for the *protein content* of the food, not for the total food. It will be noted that for some foods, the portion containing 10 grams of protein is larger than that ordinarily consumed. In some cases, this should pose no problem. One can serve three or more protein-containing foods instead of two, with lesser amounts of each. We are using a 10 gram portion merely as a device to provide accurate comparisons of the true cost of different foods.

All costs are based on the weight of the food as purchased, not as served. You pay for one pound of bacon at a certain price, on the basis of its uncooked weight. After frying, the bacon served weighs less. These differences are automatically taken care of in the table and need be of no further concern. For some foods commonly sold in units other than weight, such as eggs and milk, the price has been converted to a weight basis for our purposes. Let us now turn to more specific suggestions for the planning of meals in relation to this table.

BREAKFAST

A basic breakfast on most days would consist of fruit juice, 2 to 4 slices of toast with margarine or jelly, a serving of cooked cereal, and a beverage. Oatmeal combined with reconstituted nonfat dry milk would be the most economical source of breakfast protein. This would cost about 23% as much as the same amount of protein in bacon and eggs. In general, it will be noted that regular hot cereals are the most economical sources of breakfast protein. Next comes nonfat dry milk. Meat and eggs are quite high. It may be surprising to see how high the cost of protein in some dry cereals is. Kelloggs Special K and Grapenuts are high priced but possible sources of 10 grams of protein. Corn flakes and similar products are reasonably priced, but a virtually impossible volume—5 1/3 cups—would have to be eaten to provide 10 grams of protein. Cooked cereals other than oatmeal and Cream of Wheat are only slightly more expensive, unless they are the instant variety. Cooked cereals costing less than 40¢ per pound provide protein at a cost of less than 3.5¢ for 10 grams. Such cereals can be considered good buys. Instant cooked cereals have no more nutritional value than regular cooked cereals.

Pre-sweetened dry cereals are exceedingly expensive for their nutrient content. Excellent substitutes for dry cereals can be made from the cookies for which recipes are given here. These cookies can be crumbled and eaten with milk and fresh fruit, just like dry cereals. They are at least as tasty, more nutritious, and cost about 1/2 to 1/3 as much per pound as dry cereals.

Variety in the basic breakfast can be provided in several ways. The cooked cereal can be varied to include farina, oatmeal, whole wheat cereal, and corn grits. Fresh fruit, such as bananas, peaches, and cantaloupe in season can be sliced and added to the cereal, provided their price is less than 20¢ per pound. A portion of approximately 1 to 2 ounces would be appropriate. Canned fruits, such as applesauce, are economical additions if their price is less than 25¢ per pound. They can be added to the cereal after it is cooked, in amounts of 1 to 2 ounces. Dried fruits, such as raisins, prunes, apricots, and currants may be cooked with the cereal, and are economical additions if they cost less than 90¢ per pound. Approximately 1/2 ounce of the dried fruit may be added for each serving.

In summer, cooked cereals can be served after cooling in a

refrigerator for a few minutes, and adding reconstituted milk. Fresh fruit is a particularly appropriate addition in the summer.

As an alternative to cereal on some days, wheat cakes may be served, or French toast with syrup and margarine. It would be wise to use relatively small amounts of egg in preparing these dishes, both to keep the protein cost low, and to minimize the undesirable effects of egg on heart and blood vessels.

The syrup or molasses you usually serve with pancakes and French toast are both highly overpriced, and you would be gaining in economy to use the recipe for syrup in the recipe section.

Breakfast is also traditionally the meal at which a major part of the day's ascorbic acid (vitamin C) is taken. This is a sound arrangement. The usual source of ascorbic acid is citrus fruit. One may take oranges, grapefruit, or canned or frozen orange or grapefruit juice. In general, grapefruit have about 75% as much ascorbic acid as oranges, and about 75% as much of other nutrients. Therefore, if grapefruit cost more than 75% per pound as much as oranges, oranges are a better buy. Strawberries have a high ascorbic acid content, but the price is usually much too high for them to be a reasonable substitute. Whether to buy the fresh citrus fruit, or canned or frozen juice is largely a matter of taste. Canned orange juice has about 80% as much ascorbic acid as fresh orange juice, and if cheaper than citrus fruit, may be a good buy. For fresh orange juice, one must buy whole oranges which have slightly over 20% waste. Accordingly, in terms of the nutrient content only, fresh and canned orange juice are worth about the same per pound. One may be willing to pay somewhat more for a desirable taste. Frozen concentrate should be compared on the basis of its equivalence to canned juice.

LUNCH

In evaluating suitable luncheon foods, you can employ the same procedure that was used for breakfasts. Of course, 20 grams of protein may be too much for some people, and not enough for others, depending on their occupation and eating patterns. But if the choices are made on the basis of comparative costs, savings will result whether the lunch is to be eaten at home or taken out. For our purpose, lunches eaten in restaurants are not being considered, since the basic cost of the food eaten is only one factor involved in the total expense of restaurant eating.

Sandwiches have been the most common American lunch, but due to the rising cost of meat, the familiar meat sandwich has become quite uneconomical, and we will consider some alternatives.

Leftovers

It is common to serve leftovers from the previous dinner for lunch. This is a fine idea. However, one should not get the impression that this saves money. The leftovers cost money when they were purchased, and whether that cost is allocated to the dinner or the lunch does not change the fact that the foods were paid for. To the extent that there are leftovers, they should be served, but to deliberately prepare extra food for dinner in order to have leftovers for lunch may not be economical. If the leftovers are meat, fish, or other expensive foods, this procedure will raise food costs. If the leftovers are inexpensive foods, then some savings may result.

Sandwiches

It can be seen from the table that bread is an economical source of protein for lunch, and the bread in two sandwiches supplies slightly over half of the needed protein. An economical, highly nutritious lunch would be two peanut butter sandwiches and some fruit. Other sandwiches can be served (see recipes), and if the fillings have less protein than peanut butter, a glass of milk will make up most of the difference.

Meats and Fish

Of the meats and fish that are generally eaten for lunch, chunk style tuna fish seems to be the best buy at current prices.

Cheese

Most cheeses are expensive with the exception of cottage cheese which is economical and an excellent choice for lunch.

Spaghetti and Other Pastas

Dried spaghetti, macaroni, or noodles cooked at home are the most economical sources of protein for lunch. Served with home-made meat sauce, spaghetti would cost about 5.7¢ for 10 grams of protein, which is more economical than canned beans or even milk. A meatless sauce would involve even more saving. Canned spaghetti, on the other hand, may be more expensive than some meats and fish, since one is paying extra for the preparation.

Beans

If purchased at a low price per can, under 22¢ per pound, canned beans are a more economical dish than most meats or fish. However, dried beans are consistently a highly economical source of protein, and recipes for their preparation are given in the recipe section.

Condensed Soups

Of the common condensed soups, only two—bean with bacon (or pork) and split pea—provide protein at reasonable cost. The other soups available cannot be considered economical in relation to the small amounts of protein they contain. Whether one wishes to purchase them largely for their flavor and convenience is a personal matter. They may be worth purchasing as flavoring agents in a meat extender or meat substitute dish.

DINNER

Most people eat more at dinner than at either breakfast or lunch, but the same principles of comparison hold in relation to protein content and costs. Two kinds of foods are evaluated in the

"Protein-Cost Counter." First, there are the usual sources of protein at dinner—beef, pork, lamb, chicken, and fish. Then there are the lower cost protein-containing foods that are recommended either as extenders or as substitutes. In this way, it will be possible to judge the extent to which one can save by using these extenders and substitutes.

Within a particular category, such as choice beef, the range of costs for 10 grams of protein is at least as great as the difference in costs for most of the categories, except chicken. In the representative sample of choice beef cuts, the range of costs for 10 grams of protein is 9.8¢ to 20.9¢. The range for pork, lamb, and fish falls within these limits. This means that if prices per pound are similar, there is no significant savings in switching to pork, lamb, or fish. Contrary to many people's beliefs, *fish is not a more concentrated source of protein than trimmed beef.* This is even true of fish fillets which have no evident waste. The figures for the meats are based on the assumption that they will be trimmed of all obvious excess fat at the time of purchase. Keep in mind that the cheaper cuts of meat provide protein at a lower cost.

Chicken, at current prices, offers a slight savings over hamburger, and a significant savings over other cuts of beef, pork, lamb, and fish. This, however, applies only to whole chicken. Certain parts that are higher priced than whole chicken will not be any bargain.

Continuing to the foods that can be used as meat extenders or meat substitutes, we can see much lower prices. They provide protein at a price ranging from 5¢ to less than 1¢ for 10 grams. Some of the low-cost foods containing protein are somewhat bulky, however, and it may not be practical to eat enough of one of them to get 10 grams of protein. On the other hand, since there is usually more time for eating dinner than for breakfast or lunch, one can plan to provide the needed protein from more than two main sources. For example, lima bean and barley soup, spaghetti with sauce, a salad with cottage cheese, and a dessert topped with whipped reconstituted dry nonfat milk can supply a full amount of balanced protein at an average cost of less than 4¢

per 10 grams (about 8¢ for 20 grams, or 11¢ for 30 grams in the case of those who eat more than the average adult). This is a savings of 50 to 75 percent over conventional dinners based on meat, fish or poultry. By using the meat-extender approach, one can attain savings of 25 to 45 percent—less, but still significant.

Other Dinner Foods

Vegetables are commonly eaten at dinner, and the price of vegetables also varies widely. This variation does not reflect the true nutritional value of the different vegetables. By using the "Food-Value Counter," one can pick out the most economical vegetables and fruits.

SNACKS, DESSERTS, AND BEVERAGES

Family Snacks

Most snack foods are highly overpriced in terms of their food value. A common example is potato chips. Purchased cookies and crackers also tend to be too expensive. Baked goods costing more than 1½ times as much as bread per pound are not good buys. In general, substantial savings can result from eliminating such items.

Snacks that are eaten at home between meals should emphasize bread (or toast) with an inexpensive spread. Peanut butter or cottage cheese are excellent. Jams and jellies tend to be overpriced, but if used sparingly are acceptable. Fruits should be selected on the basis of price. Home-baked foods made from the recipes given in this book, or from your own, are nutritious and economical.

Desserts

The basic ingredient of most desserts is sugar. Indeed, in England, a dessert is called a "sweet." Although sugar is one of the least expensive foods available, many desserts tend to be overpriced. Ice cream, for example, is overpriced in relation to its nutritional value. Many of its calories come from fat and are therefore undesirable. Ice milk is a better food, but it too tends to be high in price. When some inexpensive fruits are available, they make excellent desserts. At other times, economical desserts can be prepared at home.

Beverages

Most beverages tend to be reasonably priced, but one can still save. Generally, tea is less expensive than coffee. With fresh coffee at 75¢ to $1.00 a pound, one can get 46 six-ounce cups per pound, at a cost of 1.6 to 2.2¢ per cup. Tea bags at 48 for 6¢ provide a cup of tea at 1.3¢. If one uses a tea bag for two cups of tea, which is quite practical, each cup would cost 0.65¢. Instant coffee at 55¢ for 2 oz., provides 26 cups at about 2.1¢ per cup. Instant tea, at 51¢ for one ounce provides 35 cups at 1.5¢ per cup. Clearly, tea is more economical than coffee. It may seem trivial to be concerned with saving one cent a cup, but all savings add up. A family of four may consume an average of 10 cups of some beverage per day. If one can save one cent per cup, the savings would be 10¢ per day, or $36.50 per year. Because of the multiplier effect described earlier, this really amounts to a saving of over $100 per year. The essence of a successful saving program on food is the saving at every opportunity.

Soft drinks generally cost from 2.8 to 8.4 cents for a 6 oz. portion when purchased in packages at the supermarket. Their nutritional value consists only of sugar which is worth a small fraction of the total. Therefore, if one does buy soft drinks, it is advisable to buy the least expensive. Concentrated drink syrups can produce drinks at a cost of about 2 cents for each 6 oz.

serving. This could be a saving for a large family if you are sure the syrup will be used and not wasted. Dry drink mixes such as Kool-Aid usually produce a drink costing about 1 to 1 1/2 cents for a 6 oz. serving. This is clearly a significant saving over bottled drinks.

Table II   Protein Cost Counter

Food	Portion containing 10 grams of protein		Based on price per pound	Cost of portion containing 10 grams of protein
	Grams	Household measure (approx.)		
Barley				
dried	122	4½ oz.	$ .16	under 1 ¢
Beans and Lentils				
beans, canned, Van Camps	159	5½ oz.	.19	6.3
beans, canned, vegetarian	159	5½ oz. (1 cup) or ⅓ can	.21	7.2
beans, kidney, dried	44	1½ oz.	.41	3.5
beans, large, lima, dried	44	1½ oz.	.40	3.6
beans, small, red, dried	44	1½ oz.	.21	under 1
beans, white, dried	45	1½ oz.	.24	1.3
Beef				
hamburger, regular	56		.89	9.8
hamburger, lean	48		1.09	11.1
liver	50		.92	9.9
round roast	50		1.83	18.5
T-bone steak, trimmed	68		2.05	20.9
chuck steak, without bone, trimmed	52		1.15	11.5
rib roast	68		1.39	14.2
Bread	115	3½ slices	.28	4.4

Table II Protein Cost Counter (Continued)

| Food | Portion containing 10 grams of protein | | | Cost of portion containing 10 grams of protein |
	Grams	Household measure (approx.)	Based on price per pound	
Cereals, cold				
Alpha Bits, Post	130	4½ cups	$ .69	14.3 ¢
Apple Jacks, Kelloggs	227	7½ cups	.90	33.9
Corn Flakes, Kelloggs	133	5⅓ cups	.36	5.3
Fruity Pebbles, Post	312	9 cups	.77	40.6
Grapenuts, Post	114	1 cup	.55	9.5
Rice Crispies, Kelloggs	154	5½ cups	.73	22.5
Shredded Wheat	91	2 cups	.46	8.5
Special K, Kelloggs	50	2 cups	.81	7.1
Sugar Smacks, Kelloggs	200	6½ cups	.61	13.8
Cereals, cooked				
cream of wheat (dry) or farina	88	3 oz.	.30	2.9
oatmeal, dry	70	2½ oz.	.26	1.7
Cheese				
American	40	1¼ oz.	1.19	9.2
cottage	58.8	2 oz.	.39	5.0
Eggs	78	1¼ large	.80/doz.	9.6
Fish				
cod, frozen	57		.75	9.4
halibut, sliced	48		1.49	15.7

Table II Protein Cost Counter (Continued)

Food	Portion containing 10 grams of protein			Cost of portion containing 10 grams of protein
	Grams	Household measure (approx.)	Based on price per pound	
perch fillets, frozen	51		$ .99	11.1 ¢
Fish, canned				
salmon, pink	49	1¾ oz.	.96	10
sardines in mustard sauce	53	2 oz.	.80	8.7
tuna, chunk, in water	36	1¼ oz.	.935	7.3
Flour and Grains				
cornmeal	111	4 oz.	.18	under 1
flour, rye	106	3¾ oz.	.24	2.3
flour, wheat	95	3⅓ oz.	.16	under 1
rice, long grain (not instant)	135	4¾ oz.	.22	1.7
Lamb				
chops, bone	68		1.32	14.3
Macaroni and Spaghetti				
macaroni and cheese, canned, Franco American	256	9 oz.	.24	12
macaroni, dry	80	2¾ oz.	.24	1.6
spaghetti, dry	80	2¾ oz.	.24	1.6
Meats				
bacon	119	4 oz.	.90	16.5

Table II Protein Cost Counter (Continued)

| Food | Portion containing 10 grams of protein | | | Cost of portion containing 10 grams of protein |
	Grams	Household measure (approx.)	Based on price per pound	
ham	68	2 oz.	$ .85	12.5 ¢
hamburger, regular	56	2 oz.	.89	9.8
ham, deviled	72	2¾ oz.	1.28	18
potted meat food	56	2 oz.	.70	7.8
sausage	66	2 oz.	.84	10.1
Spam	67	2½ oz.	.87	11
Milk				
dry, nonfat	28	1 oz.	.80	4.2
liquid, nonfat	277	1¾ glasses	.27/qt.	7.0
whole	286	1¾ glasses	.29/qt.	8.4
Peanut Butter	40	1¼ oz.	.61	3.0
Pork				
chops, loin	58		1.35	20.6
ham, cooked, boneless, trimmed	43		1.67	16.7
steak	58		1.22	18.5
Poultry				
chicken, fryer, whole	54		.48	8.1
chicken, roaster, whole	51		.55	8.1

Table II   Protein Cost Counter (Continued)

Food	Portion containing 10 grams of protein			Cost of portion containing 10 grams of protein
	Grams	Household measure (approx.)	Based on price per pound	
Soups				
canned, bean with pork	156	5½ oz.	.25	8.6
canned, beef noodle	313	11 oz.	.36	23
canned, condensed, chicken noodle	357	12½ oz.	.28	20
canned, split pea	143	5 oz.	.27	9.0
canned, tomato	625	22 oz. (2 cans)	.21	26
Wheat Cakes				
made with whole milk, no eggs	76 (dry wt.)	5 pancakes	.27 for flour mix	4.6
made with whole milk, 1 egg (4 servings)				6.5
made with nonfat dry milk X2, no eggs	58 (dry wt.)	3½ pancakes	.27 for flour mix	3.4
made with nonfat dry milk X2, 1 egg (4 servings)				5.3

Chapter 5

RECIPES FOR HIGH NUTRITION
AT LOW COST

The following series of recipes is presented to illustrate ways of obtaining nutritious meals inexpensively. They are not designed as fancy fare, but you should feel free to add condiments and herbs to suit your taste.

The recipes are grouped by meal and type of dish, such as main course, side dish, or dessert. A few of the recipes are adapted from government publications, and all have been tested by housewives.

If a recipe involves a substantial amount of a certain food, it should be used when that food is plentiful and inexpensive, or when the cost is not more than 25% over the fair value range.* Greater flexibility is possible when only a small amount of a fairly expensive food is called for. A good guide would be to use an auxilliary food (such as raisins) if the price doesn't exceed the fair value range by more than 50%, and if the total cost involved in serving four people is less than 20¢.

In some cases, substitutions can be made. For example, dried nonfat milk, condensed milk, and evaporated milk are interchangeable. Experimentation will help you find the correct ratio for a given dish, and you may find slight differences in taste and texture. When available, two commercial products, Eggbeaters (frozen) and Eggstra (dried) are superior to fresh eggs for most recipes.

*The fair value range for numerous foods is presented in the Food-Value Counter.

In many of the following recipes, small amounts of onion are used to improve the flavor. Onion is a food that is generally available at a reasonable cost. However, if for reasons of taste and variety, one prefers another flavoring, chopped celery, green pepper, or parsley may be substituted for onion.

A useful addition to the kitchen in terms of food preparation is a pressure cooker. It can eliminate many of the cumbersome and laborious aspects of preparing inexpensive, nutritious foods, such as dried beans. *(Never fill a pressure cooker more than ⅓ full,* including food and water. The vents could clog and cause an explosion.)

BREAKFAST RECIPES

Banana Wheatcakes

1 ½ cups flour
3 tablespoons sugar
1 teaspoon salt
3 tablespoons baking powder
2 tablespoons vegetable oil
1 cup nonfat dry milk, reconstituted at 2X regular concentration
2 eggs
2 thinly sliced bananas

Mix flour, sugar, salt and baking powder. Add oil, milk, and eggs and mix into a smooth batter. Fold in bananas. Brown on both sides in greased pan. Serve with margarine and homemade syrup for breakfast; sugar for lunch; or crushed pineapple for dinner.

Cornmeal Mush, Cooked

3 cups boiling water
1 cup cornmeal
1 cup cold water
1 teaspoon salt

Mix cornmeal, cold water, and salt. Slowly stir cornmeal mixture into the boiling water in saucepan. Cook and stir until thick. Lower heat. Cover and cook 15 minutes, stirring as needed to keep from sticking.

Cornmeal Mush, Fried

Put hot cornmeal mush (recipe above) in a loaf pan. Cool until firm. Remove mush from pan and cut into slices. Put slices of mush in heated, greased fry pan and brown on both sides. Serve with a sweet sauce (See under "Sauces and Syrups.")

Muesli, Modified (a Swiss dish for breakfast or dessert)

½ cup oatmeal
2 tablespoons sugar
1 ¼ cups water
4 tablespoons orange juice
2 bananas, sliced
1 apple (when cheap), coarsely grated
½ cup condensed milk
4 teaspoons chopped peanuts, if desired

Cook oatmeal with sugar and water. Allow to cool. Add orange juice, bananas, apples, and milk and stir to a light creamy texture. Put into individual bowls and sprinkle with chopped peanuts.

LUNCH RECIPES

Broiled Sardines on Toast

8 slices toast
2 tins sardines
2 tablespoons ketchup or mayonnaise

Spread ketchup or mayonnaise on toast slices. Add sardines, broil for 5 minutes, and serve.

Crushed Pineapple Sandwich

2 tablespoons canned, crushed pineapple—well drained
2 tablespoons mayonnaise
2 slices white or rye bread

Mix pineapple and mayonnaise. Spread on bread and cover.

Grated Cabbage and Carrot Sandwich

2 tablespoons grated raw cabbage
2 tablespoons grated raw carrot
2 tablespoons mayonnaise
2 slices white, rye or pumpernickel bread

Mix cabbage, carrot, and mayonnaise. Spread on bread and cover.

Luncheon Meat Sandwich

4 large slices rye bread, toasted and spread with margarine
1 can (12 ounces) luncheon meat, cut in 8 slices
8 slices onion
1 can (16 ounces) vegetarian beans
4 slices Swiss cheese

Top each bread slice with 2 slices meat and onion. Stir beans in can; spoon equally over each sandwich. Bake at 350° for 15 minutes. Top with cheese; return to oven to melt.

Peanut Butter and Banana Sandwich

½ banana, cut diagonally
peanut butter to taste
2 slices white or raisin bread

Spread peanut butter on bread, add banana, and cover.

DINNER RECIPES

Meat, Poultry, and Fish Extenders

Beans and Ham with Dill

1 cup ham cut in strips
¼ cup sliced onion
2 tablespoons margarine
1 can (16 ounces) beans in tomato sauce
¼ cup chopped cucumber
2 teaspoons chopped fresh dill

In saucepan, brown ham and cook onion in margarine until tender. Add remaining ingredients. Heat, stirring occasionally.

Beef Pot Pie

¼ cup barley
1 cup diced beef
1 cup diced potatoes
½ cup lima beans—fresh, canned or frozen
½ cup peas
½ cup corn
1 cup diced carrots
1 cup diced or canned tomatoes
3 beef flavored bouillon cubes
1 tablespoon minced onion
½ teaspoon salt
Pie crust No. 1 (½ recipe)

Boil barley until soft. Add beef and vegetables; cook until tender. Drain off most of water.
Add bouillon cubes, onion, and salt. Place in greased casserole and cover with pie crust. Puncture to release steam during baking.
Bake at 350° for 1 hour.

Beef-Tomato-Rice Stew

2 small onions, chopped
2 tablespoons vegetable oil
½ pound ground beef (1 cup)
3 cups cooked or canned tomatoes
½ cup uncooked rice
1 cup water
Salt and pepper, as you like

Put onions, oil, and ground beef in pan. Cook until meat is browned and onions are tender.
Add rest of ingredients. Cover and cook slowly about 25 minutes until rice is tender.

Beef Vegetable Skillet

½ pound ground beef
1 medium onion, chopped
1 can tomato soup
1 can chunky vegetable soup
1 can (20 oz.) chick peas, drained
2 teaspoons horseradish

In skillet, brown beef and cook onion until tender. (Use oil or margarine if necessary.) Stir to separate meat; pour off fat and add remaining ingredients. Heat, stirring occasionally.

Black-Eyed Pea Croquettes

2 cups dried black-eyed peas, cooked
1 cup cooked smoked ham, finely chopped
½ cup cornflakes, finely crushed
1 ½ teaspoon grated onion
1 ½ teaspoon chopped fresh parsley if desired
1 teaspoon salt
¼ teaspoon pepper
1 egg, separated
¾ cup flour
¼ cup milk

2 cups cornflakes, finely crushed
8 ounces tomato sauce

Mash peas until soft. Add ham, ½ cup cornflakes, onion, parsley, salt, pepper and egg yolk. Mix thoroughly. Using generous tablespoons of mixture, form into balls. Coat with flour. Beat egg white slightly with milk. Roll the croquettes in this, then in the remaining cornflakes. Fry in deep oil until golden brown. Drain on absorbent paper. Heat tomato sauce and pour over croquettes to serve.

Campfire Supper

2 cans (16 oz. each) vegetarian beans
1 12 ounce can luncheon meat, cut in strips
2 tablespoons hot dog relish

In saucepan, combine ingredients. Heat, stir, and serve.

Chicken à la King

½ cup water
¾ pound diced fresh chicken
1 can cream of chicken soup
½ cup cooked peas
½ cup diced tomatoes
½ cup green pepper (when cheap)
1 teaspoon minced onion
Salt to taste
8 slices toast

Pressure cook chicken in ½ cup water for 15 minutes.
Add soup, peas, tomatoes, pepper, onion, and salt. Simmer 15 minutes without pressure.
Serve over 2 slices toast per person.

Chicken Casserole

¾ pound cooked or canned chicken (1 ½ cups)
1 cup cooked rice

½ cup bread crumbs
2 teaspoons minced onion
1 can condensed cream of chicken soup
3 slices tomato or green pepper

Cook chicken (if fresh) for 15 minutes in pressure cooker. Dice.
Boil rice until tender and drain.
Add chicken, rice, bread crumbs, and onion to casserole dish.
Mix in soup. Top with tomato or green pepper slices, and bake at 350°
for 30 minutes.

Chicken Gumbo

1 cup water
¾ pound chicken, cooked and diced
½ pound okra
1 can corn
1 tablespoon corn meal
1 can tomatoes
4 slices onion
4 medium potatoes, cut into sections
Salt to taste

Bring to boil mixture of chicken, okra, corn, corn meal, and tomatoes.
Lower heat.
Brown onion in skillet and add to mixture. Cook potatoes separately,
and add to mixture. Cook for 10 minutes.

Chili Con Carne Skillet

½ pound ground beef
1 medium onion, chopped
2 teaspoons chili powder
1 can tomato soup
2 cans (15 ½ oz. each) kidney beans, drained

In skillet, brown beef and cook onion with chili until tender. (Use oil or
margarine if necessary.) Stir to separate meat. Add soup and beans.
Cook over low heat 10 minutes. Stir occasionally.

Corned Beef and Bean Pan Dish

1 can (16 ounces) beans in tomato sauce
1 can cubed canned corned beef
2 tablespoons finely chopped celery
¼ teaspoon prepared horseradish
½ cup bread crumbs

In saucepan, combine ingredients. Heat, stirring occasionally. Add water as needed.

Fish and Vegetable Casserole

½ pound fish
1 cup carrots, diced
1 cup peas
1 cup lima beans
½ cup corn
½ cup tomatoes
½ cup nonfat milk—reconstituted at 3X regular concentration
Onion to taste
Salt to taste
2 teaspoons grated cheese
2 tablespoons vegetable oil

Broil fish in oil. Cut into small pieces. Meanwhile, boil vegetables in water to cover until tender. Pour off excess water. Mix fish and vegetables together, add salt and onion, and place in baking dish. Pour the skimmed milk over top. Bake for 20 minutes. Add grated cheese to top and bake for 10 more minutes.

Garden Salmon Sandwiches

7 ¾ ounce can salmon
¾ cup cottage cheese
2 tablespoons chopped parsley
½ cup chopped cucumber
2 tablespoons grated carrot
1 tablespoon chopped chives or green onions

¼ cup mayonnaise-type dressing
Salt and pepper to taste
12 slices dark bread, spread with margarine

Drain and flake salmon. Combine with cheese, vegetables,
mayonnaise-type dressing and salt and pepper. Spread half the bread
slices with salmon mixture. Top with another slice. Cut in half and
garnish with carrot curls and parsley. Makes 6 sandwiches.
Also good as a stuffing for tomatoes or as a salad with lettuce.

Ham and Bean Pie

Pie crust No. 1
1 cup cooked ham, diced
1 can beans
½ cup tomatoes—fresh or canned
1 teaspoon minced onion
½ cup carrot, sliced
2 tablespoons rye flour

Line pie dish with dough. Mix other ingredients and place in dough.
Cover with pie dough, and puncture with fork. Bake at 350° until crust
is flaky (about 45 minutes).

Ham and Lima Beans

1 cup white, dry lima beans
8 ounces cooked, diced ham (1 cup)
2 teaspoons minced onion
½ cup fresh or canned tomatoes
¼ teaspoon salt
Water

Pressure cook lima beans for 45 minutes. Pour off all but ½ cup liquid.
Add ham, onion, tomatoes, and salt. Simmer without pressure 5 to 10
minutes, stirring gently.

Ham Bake, Midwestern Style

1 ½ cups cooked ham, cut in ½-inch strips

¼ cup chopped onion
2 tablespoons margarine
2 cans (16 ounces each) beans in tomato sauce
1 cup cubed apple
⅓ cup raisins
2 teaspoons prepared mustard

In saucepan, brown ham and cook onion in margarine until onion is tender. In 1 ½ quart casserole, combine all ingredients. Cover, bake at 350° for 30 minutes. Uncover and stir. Bake 5 minutes more or until hot. Garnish with fruit if desired.

Ham South Pacific

4 cups water
1 cup blackeye peas, dried
1 cup long grain rice, uncooked
½ pound (1 cup) ham—cooked, diced
½ can crushed pineapple
¼ cup celery, diced (if cheap)
2 tablespoons corn grits or cornmeal
1 tablespoon vegetable oil

Pressure cook blackeye peas in 2 cups water for 7 minutes. Release pressure. Add rice and remaining 2 cups water and pressure cook 5 more minutes. Add other ingredients and simmer without pressure for 10 minutes while stirring from time to time. Add more water as needed.

Ham Supreme

1 cup diced cooked ham
1 tablespoon chopped onion
2 tablespoons margarine
2 cans (16 ounces each) beans in tomato sauce
½ teaspoon Worcestershire, if desired

In saucepan, brown ham and cook onion in margarine until tender.
Add beans and Worcestershire. Heat, stirring occasionally. If desired, garnish with canned peaches or pineapple, orange sections, or chopped apple.

Holiday Meat and Beans

2 cans (16 ounces each) beans with tomato sauce
¼ cup finely chopped celery
Dash cinnamon
1 can (12 ounce) luncheon meat, cut in 6 slices
2 tablespoons cranberry-orange relish or orange marmalade

In shallow baking dish, combine beans, celery, and cinnamon. Top with meat, spread with relish. Bake at 400° for 20 minutes or until hot.

Mackerel-Potato Cakes

1 can mackerel (15 ounces)
½ small onion, chopped
1 ½ cups cold, mashed potatoes
1 egg
½ teaspoon salt
Pepper, if desired
Oil for frying

Drain mackerel. Break fish in small pieces. Put in large bowl. Add onion, potatoes, egg, salt, and pepper. Mix well. Shape into 12 cakes. Heat oil in fry pan. Fry cakes over medium heat 3 to 4 minutes until browned on one side. Turn gently and fry 3 to 4 minutes on other side (until browned). Drain well.

Meat Loaf

1 medium onion
1 stalk celery
1 egg
1 cup ground beef (½ pound)
¾ cup cooked, quick rolled oats
½ cup tomato sauce
1 teaspoon salt
¼ teaspoon pepper

Finely chop onion and celery.
Mix all ingredients well. Shape into a loaf in a baking pan.
Bake at 350° about 1 hour until browned.

Meat Sauce

1 medium-sized onion
1 tablespoon oil
1 cup cut-up canned chopped meat or canned luncheon meat
¾ cup tomato paste (6-ounce can)
1 ½ cups water
1 teaspoon sugar
Salt to taste

Chop onion. Cook in oil until tender.
Mix in rest of ingredients. Cook slowly about 45 minutes until thickened.
Serve meat sauce over hot cooked rice, noodles, or spaghetti.

Paella Banana

1 cup diced chicken
1 onion, chopped
½ cup lima beans, frozen
3 tablespoons oil
3 bananas, sliced
1 cup long grain rice, cooked
½ cup tomato, raw or canned—diced
½ teaspoon paprika
1 teaspoon salt
¼ cup water (about)

Lightly brown chicken and onion in oil. Place in pot. Add other ingredients. Simmer for 20 minutes, adding more water if necessary.

Quick Deep Dish Salmon Pie

1 can pea soup (10 ½ ounce)
½ pound can salmon
½ cup milk
1 cup cooked, sliced potatoes
½ cup sliced onion
⅛ teaspoon white pepper
⅛ teaspoon oregano
⅛ teaspoon sweet basil
1 package refrigerator buttermilk biscuits

In saucepan, combine soup, liquid from can of salmon, and the milk. Stir in salmon, poatoes, onions and seasonings. Heat until sauce begins to simmer, stirring occasionally. Empty into a 2-quart casserole or baking dish. Top with biscuits. Bake in preheated 400° oven for 15 to 20 minutes, or until biscuits are brown.

Rice and Beans, with Meat

2 cups cooked dry beans
2 cups water
1 cup cut-up canned luncheon meat
1 cup uncooked rice
Salt and pepper to taste

Put beans, meat, rice and water in a pan. Bring to boiling. Lower heat. Cover and boil gently about 25 minutes until rice is tender. Add salt and pepper, and serve.

Salmon Biscuit Roll with Lemon Sauce

½ cup chopped celery
¼ cup minced onion
2 tablespoons margarine
½ pound can salmon
10 ½-ounce cream of chicken soup
2 cups biscuit mix
⅔ cup milk
1 egg
1 tablespoon water

Saute celery and onion in margarine until soft. Drain salmon, reserving liquid. Flake salmon and add to vegetable mixture. Stir in ¼ cup of the chicken soup. Set aside remaining soup for the sauce. Combine biscuit mix and milk. Turn out on lightly floured board and knead gently, about 12 kneading strokes. Roll dough out into a rectangle about 9 x 12 inches. Spread dough with salmon mixture and roll up lengthwise, like a jelly roll. Transfer roll to baking sheet, seam side down. Combine egg and water. Brush roll with egg mixture. Bake in preheated 400° oven for 25 to 35 minutes, or until lightly browned. Serve hot with Chicken Lemon Sauce. To make sauce, add sufficient milk to reserved salmon liquid to measure ½ cup liquid. Combine this liquid with remaining chicken soup. Add 1 to 2 tablespoons lemon juice, or to taste. Heat to serving temperature.

Salmon-Cornbread Ring

1 tablespoon minced onion
½ cup diced tomato
2 tablespoons vegetable oil
½ pound can salmon
Milk
1 egg, lightly beaten
1 cup corn muffin mix

Saute onion and tomato until tender. Drain salmon liquid and add milk to make ¾ cup liquid. Stir liquid and egg into muffin mix. Stir in vegetable mixture. Oil an 8 cup ring mold. Line bottom with waxed paper. Oil paper. Flake salmon and sprinkle in bottom of pan. Spoon muffin mixture over salmon. Bake at 375° for 55 minutes or until bread tests done. Cool for 5 minutes and unmold. Fill with favorite cooked vegetable. Serve with mushroom sauce.

Salmon Macaroni Salad

8 ounces elbow macaroni
1 small onion, finely chopped
¼ cup chopped parsley
1 cucumber, sliced
½ pound can salmon, drained, and flaked
1 ½ teaspoons salt
¼ teaspoon pepper
½ teaspoon dry mustard
1 ½ tablespoons vinegar
4 tablespoons salad oil
Raw cabbage leaves

Cook macaroni according to package directions. Drain. Combine macaroni with remaining ingredients, except cabbage leaves. Line large salad bowl with cabbage leaves, and empty salad into center.

Salmon Vegetable Paella

⅓ cup margarine
1 medium onion, chopped
1 clove garlic, minced
2 stalks celery, chopped
2 cups sliced summer squash, zucchini, or diced carrots
3 tomatoes, quartered, or 1 pound can whole tomatoes, drained
1 ½ cups rice, uncooked
½ pound can salmon
2 cups water or chicken broth
¼ teaspoon salt
¼ teaspoon pepper
1 cup peas

In heavy saucepan, melt margarine. In it saute onion, garlic, and celery for 5 minutes, or until onion is tender. Add summer squash, or zucchini, or diced carrots, and tomatoes. Cover tightly and cook over low heat for 10 minutes. Add rice and stir until rice is well coated with juices in pan. Add liquid from can of salmon, water or chicken broth, salt and pepper. Bring liquid to a rapid boil. Cover tightly, turn heat to very low and cook for 30 minutes. Fluff mixture with a fork. Flake and add salmon. Cover and steam for 5 minutes. Meanwhile heat peas in liquid. Drain. Empty salmon vegetable paella into serving dish and garnish with peas.

Southwest Meatballs

½ pound ground beef
1 egg, slightly beaten
3 tablespoons bread crumbs
1 tablespoon minced onion
1 teaspoon chili powder
½ teaspoon salt
1 tablespoon margarine
1 can (16 ounces) beans in tomato sauce

Combine beef, eggs, crumbs, onion, chili powder and salt. Shape into 12 meatballs. In skillet, brown meatballs in margarine. Cover, and cook over low heat 15 minutes. Stir in beans and simmer for 10 more minutes. Add water as needed. Serve.

Spaghetti Burger Skillet

½ pound ground beef
1 medium onion, chopped
1 tablespoon oregano leaves, crushed
1 can tomato bisque soup
1 can (12 oz.) tomato juice
1 soup can water
¼ pound uncooked thin spaghetti, broken in pieces

In skillet, brown beef and cook onion with oregano until tender. (Use oil or margarine if necessary.) Stir to separate meat; pour off fat. Add remaining ingredients; bring to boil. Cover, cook over low heat 20 minutes or until spaghetti is done. Stir often. Serve with grated Parmesan cheese if desired.

Split Pea and Beef Casserole

1 small onion
2 tablespoons oil
1 egg
2 cups water
2 ½ cups cooked split peas
1 cup uncooked, quick rolled wheat or rolled oats
¾ cup cut-up chopped meat or canned luncheon meat
½ teaspoon salt
Pepper, if desired

Chop onion and cook in oil until tender.
Beat egg in a large bowl and add water.
Stir onion and rest of ingredients into mixture. Pour in greased baking pan. Bake at 350° about 50 minutes.

Spudry Pie

¾ pound ground beef
1 teaspoon minced onion
1 cup diced carrots
2 cups boiled potatoes, sliced
Pie crust No. 1

Brown ground beef and onions together. Boil carrots until tender. Mix sliced potatoes, beef, onions and carrots. Make pie crust for double crust pie (Pie Crust No. 1). Place bottom crust in pie plate. Add meat mixture and top with salt and pepper. Add top crust and seal. Bake at 350° for 1 hour. (Cut slits in top of pie crust before baking.)

Stuffed Cabbage

8 large cabbage leaves
1 cup (½ pound) chopped lean beef
1 cup cooked rice
1 teaspoon salt
½ cup bread crumbs
1 tablespoon minced onion
2 tablespoons wheat flour

Soak cabbage leaves in hot water until soft enough to handle. Mix other ingredients.
Divide into 8 parts. Shape into cylinders and wrap cabbage leaves around each. Secure with toothpick. Roll in flour.
Place in oiled baking dish and bake in slow oven for 1 hour.
Baste frequently.

Stuffed Peppers

4 to 6 peppers (when cheap)
½ pound cooked fish OR ½ pound cooked chicken
1 cup cooked rice
1 cup tomatoes
2 tablespoons corn meal
2 tablespoons vegetable oil
2 slices onion, to taste
Salt to taste

Cut tops off peppers and clean out interiors. Boil until soft in water to cover. Mix other ingredients. Stuff into peppers and bake for 30 minutes at 350°.

Tamale Pie

2 ½ cups water
1 cup yellow corn meal
½ teaspoon salt
¼ teaspoon pepper
6 tablespoons vegetable oil
¼ cup onion, chopped
1 cup chopped beef, or ground beef
1 can condensed tomato soup (10 ounces)
½ tablespoon chili powder

Add ¾ cup water to corn meal to make mush. Boil remaining water, and add mush, salt and pepper, stirring frequently over low heat until thick. Remove from heat, add three tablespoons of oil and stir. Heat remaining oil in large skillet and brown onions and meat. Add tomato soup and chili powder. Cook 10 minutes. Put half the cooked corn meal in casserole. Add meat mixture and cover with remaining corn meal. Bake at 400° for 25-30 minutes.

Tuna and Macaroni

2 cups hot, cooked macaroni
¼ small onion
1 chicken bouillon cube, if you like
3 tablespoons flour
½ teaspoon salt
2 cups nonfat dry milk, reconstituted at 2X regular concentration
1 can chunk tuna (6½ to 7 ounces)

Leave drained macaroni in pan. Chop onion and bouillon cube (if used). Add to macaroni. Mix the flour and salt with a little of the milk until smooth. Stir rest of milk and the flour mixture in with the macaroni. Cook and stir gently until thickened. Add tuna. Heat, stirring to keep from sticking.

DINNER RECIPES

No Meat, Poultry, or Fish
(Including Sauces for Main Dishes)

Barley Loaf

1 cup barley
2 cups cabbage, grated
½ cup raisins
1 cup tomatoes, diced—raw or canned
½ cup lima beans, frozen
4 tablespoons oil
½ teaspoon salt OR garlic salt
¼ cup water (1 ½ cups if pressure cooked)

Cook or pressure cook barley until soft. Drain. Add other ingredients
and mix. Place in a pan that has a thin layer of cooking oil, and bake at
300° for 30 minutes. Serve plain or with a sauce.

Bean Loaf

9 ounces (1 ⅛ cups) cooked lima or white beans, drained
1 package instant chicken broth
¼ teaspoon rubbed sage
½ teaspoon dehydrated onion flakes
Dash garlic powder
1 teaspoon Worchestershire sauce
½ cup tomato juice
½ cup cooked diced celery
½ medium green pepper (if cheap), diced
2 ounces cooked diced carrots
Salt and pepper to taste
½ medium tomato, sliced

Preheat oven to 400°. Mix first 7 ingredients and blend in blender. Fold
in next 3 ingredients. Season. Place in small loaf pan, arrange tomato

slices on top and bake for 45 minutes. Serves 2 as main dish, or 4 as side dish.

Bean Pie

1 cup dry beans (any type)
2 beef bouillon cubes
1 tablespoon minced onion
2 tablespoons vegetable oil
6 ounce can tomato paste
1 tablespoon vinegar
2 tablespoons sugar
½ cup chopped celery
Garlic salt to taste
Pie Crust No. 1

Put beans and bouillon cubes in pressure cooker and pressure cook according to package directions. Drain. Saute onion in oil. Drain. To beans add tomato paste, vinegar, sugar, onion, and celery. Mix while heating. Add garlic salt to taste. Place in pie crust and bake at 350° until light brown. Serves 4 to 6.

Blackeye Pie

1 cup blackeye peas, dry
¼ cup canned crushed pineapple
½ cup carrots, diced
¼ teaspoon oregano
½ teaspoon salt
Pie crust No. 1

Pressure cook blackeye peas for 20 minutes. Relieve pressure. Add pineapple and carrots and cook for 5 minutes. Drain. Add oregano and salt and mix. Place in pie crust and cover with top crust. Bake at 350° 45 minutes to 1 hour or until crust is golden brown.

Cold Vegetable Meal

Note: This is suitable for warm weather. Out of the vegetables listed, choose 5 or more, depending on cost and preference. The vitamin content of this meal is much higher than that of most meals. Therefore, it may be worthwhile to serve this meal once a week in order to keep the vitamin levels at a high level. (It is recommended that about six slices per adult of various breads accompany this meal.)

1 cup beets, sliced
1 cup onion, sliced
1 ½ cups carrots
1 ½ cups cabbage, grated
⅓ head cauliflower
1 green pepper
4 stalks celery
2 large tomatoes, sliced
1 large cucumber, sliced
1 cup cottage cheese
5 tablespoons French OR Italian Dressing
8 tablespoons mayonnaise
5 tablespoons Russian dressing
5 tablespoons vinegar
½ cup prune sauce (allow 30 min. to make)
White bread, whole wheat bread, rye bread, raisin bread, pumpernickel, and corn bread
Salt

Boil beets and carrots until tender. Remove from pot and place in refrigerator. Boil cauliflower until almost tender and place in refrigerator. As they are cooling, slice other vegetables. Each vegetable with its dressing should be served on a separate platter or bowl. When beets are cold, slice thinly, and add half of the sliced onion. Place in bowl and add vinegar, mixing gently. Cut cauliflower into bite-size chunks. Place on a platter and add French or Italian dressing. Mix grated cabbage with mayonnaise. Place sliced tomato and green pepper on platter, and cover lightly with half a cup of cottage cheese. On top of cottage cheese, put 2 tablespoons Russian dressing, and salt lightly. Mix remaining cottage cheese and 3 tablespoons Russian dressing and use to stuff celery. Prepare prune sauce (see recipe) and pour over sliced carrots. Refrigerate all dishes. A suggested serving sequence is given below, with accompanying breads.

1. Stuffed celery—rye bread or pumpernickel
2. Cauliflower with French or Italian dressing—white or rye bread
3. Carrots with prune sauce—white or corn bread
4. Grated cabbage with mayonnaise—white or whole wheat bread
5. Sliced beets and onion—pumpernickel, rye or white bread
6. Sliced cucumber and Russian dressing or mayonnaise—pumpernickel or rye bread
7. Tomato and green pepper with mayonnaise—whole wheat or white bread

Dry Beans or Peas

2 cups dry beans or peas
Water: 5 cups water for small red, Great Northern, lima, or blackeye peas
6 cups water for kidney, pinto (navy), or small white peas
2 teaspoons salt

Wash and drain beans. For **Regular Method,** put beans and water in large pan and let stand 1 hour. Add salt and boil beans gently until tender. Add more water if needed. To **Pressure Cook,** put beans, salt, and water in pressure cooker and cook specified time. May be served plain or with a sauce. Approximate cooking times are listed below.

	Regular Method (hours)	Pressure Cooking (minutes)
Kidney, pinto, and pea (navy)	2	45 to 60
Small red and small white	1 ½	45
Great Northern	1 ¼	35 to 45
Lima	1	25 to 35
Blackeye peas	½	12

Fried Bananas

½ cup very fine bread crumbs
½ cup corn grits OR corn meal

1 large egg
⅓ cup nonfat dry milk, reconstituted at 3X regular concentration
½ teaspoon salt
6 bananas, sliced at angle, 1 inch thick
Oil for frying

Mix corn grits and bread crumbs. Mix beaten egg, milk, and salt, and beat slightly. Dip banana slices in egg and milk mixture, and roll in bread and cornmeal mixture. Deep fry until brown. Drain and serve hot. Good with a little peanut butter sauce.

Fried Beans and Rice

1 cup dry beans, any type, pressure cooked according to package directions
1 cup rice, cooked (not instant)
1 teaspoon minced onion
2 teaspoons oil
Garlic salt to taste
1 small can tomato paste mixed with ½ envelope dried onion soup mix
¼ cup grated cheddar cheese
Water

Put beans and cooked rice into skillet along with minced onion, oil, and garlic salt. Brown rice slightly. Add tomato paste and onion soup mix, and about ¼ cup water. Simmer for 10 minutes. Garnish with grated cheese.

Savory Beans

1 cup large lima beans, dry
½ cup corn grits
¼ cup onion, chopped or grated
Salt to taste
Water

Pressure cook lima beans for 25 minutes. Relieve pressure and drain, leaving about 1 cup of water. Add corn grits and cook for 2 more minutes under pressure. Drain. Add onions and salt, and mix. Simmer gently for 5 minutes.

Spaghetti or Macaroni

2 cups uncooked spaghetti or macaroni
1 teaspoon salt
6 cups water

Add salt to water in a large pan. Heat to boiling. Stir in spaghetti or macaroni. Boil 10 to 14 minutes until tender. Drain off cooking water. Makes 4 cups.

Succotash Loaf

1 10-ounce package frozen succotash
1 cup oatmeal
2 cups water
½ teaspoon salt
1 tablespoon vegetable oil
1 teaspoon minced onion

Cook oatmeal according to package directions. Add oil. Fold in succotash (cooked) and bake for 30 minutes at 350°. Serve with mushroom sauce or onion sauce.

Texas Beans

½ cup sliced celery
½ cup chopped onion
2 small cloves garlic, minced
½ teaspoon chili powder
4 tablespoons margarine
2 cans (16 ounces each) beans in tomato sauce
1 cup whole kernel corn
Shredded lettuce or cabbage

In saucepan, cook celery, onion, garlic and chili powder in margarine until celery is tender. Add beans and corn. Heat, stirring occasionally. Garnish with lettuce or cabbage.

Top of Stove Beans

5 cups cooked pea (navy) beans, or lima beans
½ cup sugar
2 tablespoons vegetable oil
2 tablespoons prepared mustard
¾ cup tomato sauce
Salt, pepper, and minced onion if desired
Water

Drain beans. Mix beans and rest of ingredients in a pan. Cover and boil gently about 30 minutes to blend flavors. Add a little water if sauce gets too thick.

Western Beans

1 cup baby lima beans, dry
½ cup corn, frozen
½ cup tomato, diced—canned or raw
Onion salt to taste

Pressure cook lima beans for 20 minutes. Relieve pressure. Add corn and cook for 3 minutes. Add tomato and onion salt and mix. Simmer for 5 minutes.

Western Bean Pie

1 cup dry baby limas
½ cup frozen corn
½ cup diced tomato
1 teaspoon minced onion
Salt to taste
Pie crust No. 1

Pressure cook beans for 20 minutes. Relieve pressure. Add corn and cook for another 3 minutes. Add tomato, onion, salt, and simmer until onion is reconstituted. Place in pie dough, cover with top crust and bake at 350° for 45 minutes. Serves 4.

Sauces

Cheese Sauce

1 cup nonfat milk, reconstituted at 2X regular concentration
4 ounces sharp cheddar cheese
¼ teaspoon garlic salt
½ sliced tomato

Bring milk to a boil. Add shredded cheese and stir until melted. Add garlic salt. Serve over cooked macaroni or mix with macaroni and bake at 375° until top browns. Top with sliced tomato.

Chicken Sauce for Noodles and Spaghetti

1 can condensed cream of chicken soup
1 teaspoon minced onion
½ cup diced tomato
¼ teaspoon salt

Mix all ingredients and heat until tomato is tender. Serve over cooked noodles. Suitable also for lunch.

Mushroom Sauce

1 can condensed mushroom soup
1 tablespoon whole wheat OR rye flour
½ cup water
1 tablespoon oil

Mix ingredients and heat to simmering point. Remove from heat, and serve. Makes 2 cups of sauce or gravy.

Onion Sauce No. 1

1 small chopped onion
2 tablespoons margarine

2 tablespoons flour
1 cup milk, regular or reconstituted dry nonfat at 2X regular concentration
Salt and pepper to taste

Chop onion and cook in margarine until tender. Stir in flour. Add milk slowly, stirring until smooth. Cook and stir until thickened. Add salt and pepper to season, if you wish.

Onion Sauce No. 2

4 tablespoons oil
2 large or 3 medium onions, sliced
Salt to taste
1 tablespoon flour
¼ cup water

Place oil in skillet and add onions and salt. Cover skillet and cook at low temperature until onions just begin to brown. Add flour and water, stir, and keep on stove for 5 more minutes, or until thickened. Place in serving utensil.

Spaghetti Sauce No. 1

1 medium onion, diced
2 tablespoons oil
2 cans tomato paste
Equal amount of water, or less, depending on thickness desired
½ teaspoon salt
*2 tablespoons flour
½ teaspoon minced garlic, if desired
½ teaspoon oregano, if desired

Saute onion in oil until slightly brown. Add other ingredients.
*If you have time to simmer 2 hours, omit flour.

Spaghetti Sauce No. 2

1 tablespoon minced onion
4 tablespoons vegetable oil

6 tablespoons ketchup
½ teaspoon salt
6 tablespoons water
¼ teaspoon oregano
4 tablespoons soy flour

Saute onion in oil until brown. Mix in ketchup. Add salt, water and oregano, and mix. Add soy flour to thicken.

Western Sauce for Spaghetti

1 tablespoon minced onion
2 tablespoons oil
1 can beans
1 small tomato, diced
3 tablespoons ketchup
Salt to taste

Saute onion in oil. Add all ingredients and place in blender to make sauce. Reheat and serve over spaghetti.

DINNER RECIPES

Side Dishes

Calico Slaw

½ small head cabbage
1 medium-sized turnip
2 medium-sized carrots
½ green pepper
1 green onion
1 medium-sized apple

Finely chop or thinly slice the vegetables and apple. Put in bowl. Pour

salad dressing over mixture in bowl. Mix lightly. Chill 1 hour before
serving, if desired.

Colcannon

3 cups cabbage, shredded
2 carrots, diced
4 medium potatoes, diced
1 turnip, diced
2 tablespoons vegetable oil
Salt and pepper to taste

Pressure cook all vegetables until tender (about 10 minutes). Add oil,
salt, and pepper. Serves 4 to 6.

Cooked Corn Grits

1 cup uncooked corn grits
1 teaspoon salt
4 cups water

Heat salt and water to boiling. Slowly pour and stir corn grits into
boiling water. Lower heat and stir until thickened. Cover and cook
slowly 15 minutes, stirring as needed to keep from sticking.

Cooked Dry Split Peas

1 cup dry split peas
2 cups water
½ teaspoon salt

Wash and drain split peas. Put split peas and water in a pan. Bring to
boiling. Boil 2 minutes. Remove from heat. Cover and let soak ½ hour.
Add salt, bring to boiling, cover and boil gently about 20 minutes until
tender. Do not stir.

Cooked Rice

1 cup uncooked rice

½ teaspoon salt
2 cups water

Add salt to water and heat to boiling. Stir in rice. Lower heat. Cover and cook 20 minutes. Remove from heat. Let stand 10 minutes.

Corn Fritters

1 can corn (whole kernel), drained
1 egg, beaten
1 cup nonfat dry milk, reconstituted at 2X regular concentration
¾ teaspoon salt
1 ½ cups flour, sifted

Put corn through blender until smooth. Add beaten egg, milk, and salt. Fold in sifted flour. Cook on griddle in light amount of oil until golden on both sides. Serve with syrup.

Cucumber Relish

2 cucumbers (when cheap)
2 small or 1 medium onion
⅓ cup vinegar
3 tablespoons sugar
1 cup water
Salt and pepper to taste

Peel cucumbers and slice thinly. Slice onions thinly. Mix vinegar, sugar, water, salt and pepper, and pour over the cucumbers and onion. Stir gently. Refrigerate for one hour and serve.

Fried Apples

2 medium apples, sliced ½ inch thick
1 egg
1 cup nonfat dry milk, reconstituted at 2X usual concentration
2 tablespoons, plus 4 tablespoons vegetable oil
1 tablespoon sugar
¼ teaspoon salt
½ to ¾ cup flour (enough to give proper consistency to batter)

Peel, core, and slice apples. Mix egg, nonfat reconstituted milk, two tablespoons of oil, sugar, salt and flour to form a batter. Heat the remaining 4 tablespoons of oil in frying pan. Coat each apple slice in batter and fry at about 375° for 10 minutes.
OR fry in Teflon coated pan at 350°. Serve sprinkled with cinnamon.

Fried Corn Grits

Put thick, cooked corn grits in a loaf pan. (See "Cooked Corn Grits".) Chill. Remove grits from pan and cut in slices. Put slices of corn grits in heated, greased fry pan and brown on both sides.

Glazed Carrots and Raisins

6 medium-sized carrots, cooked and cut up
½ cup carrot liquid OR water
2 tablespoons margarine
½ cup raisins
2 tablespoons sugar
Put all ingredients in pan. Cook slowly and stir gently, as needed, until carrots are hot and most of liquid is gone.

Golden Garden Bake

1 small bunch (about 2 pounds) broccoli, cooked, OR
1 medium head (about 2 pounds) cauliflower, cooked
1 can (11 ounces) cheddar cheese soup
¼ cup milk
Dash nutmeg
2 tablespoons buttered bread crumbs

In shallow baking dish, arrange vegetable. Blend soup, milk, and nutmeg. Pour over vegetable. Top with crumbs. Bake at 350° for 20 minutes or until hot.

Potato-Cheese Scallop

1 can (11 ounces) cheddar cheese soup

½ cup milk
4 cups thinly sliced potatoes
½ cup thinly sliced onion
1 tablespoon margarine
Paprika

In bowl, blend soup and milk. In 1 ½ quart casserole lined with margarine, arrange alternate layers of potatoes, onion, and sauce. Dot top with margarine; sprinkle with paprika. Cover, bake at 375° for 1 hour. Uncover, bake 15 minutes more or until potatoes are done.

Potato Pancakes No. 1

2 cups raw, grated, drained potatoes
1 egg
1 medium, grated onion
¼ teaspoon baking powder
1 tablespoon flour
Salt and pepper to taste

Mix ingredients thoroughly. Pour one tablespoonful at a time onto hot skillet or frying pan which has been coated with cooking oil. Turn and brown on both sides. Serve with apple sauce.

Potato Pancakes No. 2

Use same mixture as for potato pudding, and add ½ teaspoon of baking powder. Deep fry in oil, by tablespoonful.

Potato Pudding

2 lbs. potatoes
1 tablespoon flour
2 medium eggs or "Eggbeater"
2 ounces margarine or oil
½ teaspoon salt
Pinch of pepper
1 small onion

Peel potatoes. Grate fine. Add flour, eggs, margarine or oil, salt, and pepper. Grate onion and add. Mix thoroughly. Grease baking pan and add mixture. Bake at 350° for one hour. Cut into wedges and serve with applesauce.

Roman Style Beans

1 can (16 ounces) home style vegetarian beans
½ cup green pepper strips (when cheap)
¼ teaspoon oregano leaves, crushed
1 tablespoon margarine
Parmesan cheese

In saucepan, cook green pepper with oregano in margarine until tender. Add beans. Heat, stirring occasionally. Serve with Parmesan cheese.

Spiced Beans

1 can (16 ounces) vegetarian beans
1 can (8 ¾ ounces) fruit cocktail, drained
¼ cup celery, finely chopped
¼ teaspoon nutmeg
Toasted brown bread

In saucepan, combine all ingredients except bread. Heat, stirring occasionally. Serve with bread.

Split Pea Patties

2 ½ cups cooked split peas (see recipe)
½ small onion
1 egg
1 cup corn grits
½ cup fluid or nonfat dry milk reconstituted at 2X regular concentration
½ teaspoon salt

Mash split peas with a fork. Chop onion finely. Beat egg. Mix all ingredients. Shape into 8 patties. Chill 1 hour. Cook patties in a heated, greased fry pan until browned on both sides.

Sweet and Sour Beets

½ cup sugar
2 tablespoons flour
1 teaspoon salt
Pepper, if desired
¼ cup vinegar
½ cup beet liquid OR water
2 cups drained, cooked or canned beets

Mix sugar, flour, salt and pepper in pan. Mix in vinegar. Add beet liquid or water. Cook and stir over medium heat until mixture is thickened. Add beets and heat.

Texas Caviar

2 cans black-eyed peas
½ cup salad oil
¼ cup wine vinegar
½ clove garlic
¼ cup thinly sliced onions
½ teaspoon salt
Dash freshly ground pepper

Drain peas. Combine with oil, vinegar, onions, salt and pepper in bowl. Cover and store in refrigerator for one day. Add minced garlic. Serve on crisp bread or crackers.

Vegetables in Cream Sauce

2 tablespoons margarine
2 tablespoons flour
1 cup nonfat dry milk, reconstituted at 2X regular concentration
Salt and pepper to taste
2 cups drained, cooked or canned vegetables (carrots, peas, lima beans, or spinach)

Heat margarine, stir in flour. Add milk slowly, stirring until smooth. Cook and stir until mixture is thickened. Add salt and pepper and vegetable. Heat.

Vegetables in Peanut Butter Sauce

Use recipe for Vegetables in Cream Sauce. Add 2 tablespoons peanut butter with the margarine in making sauce. Thin the sauce with water, if you like.

Vegetables with Spices

Broccoli—Good with dill, tarragon, mustard seed
Carrots—Good with allspice, mint, bay leaves, marjoram, mace
Peas—Good with mint, basil, oregano, rosemary, sage
Spinach—Good with basil, mace, nutmeg
Green beans—Good with basil, dill, marjoram, thyme, oregano

BAKED GOODS

Banana Bread

½ cup sugar
¼ cup oil
1 ¾ cups sifted flour
1 teaspoon baking powder
½ teaspoon baking soda
½ teaspoon salt
1 cup mashed bananas
1 egg

Cream sugar and oil. Add egg and beat well. Sift dry ingredients together. Add to creamed mixture alternating with bananas. Fill greased 9x5x3 pan and bake at 350° for 45 to 50 minutes or until done. Cool on rack, wrap and store overnight before using.

Banana Cake No. 1

1 ¾ cups flour
1 tablespoon baking powder

½ teaspoon salt
¾ cup sugar
½ cup margarine
2 eggs
2 cups mashed bananas

Mix flour, baking powder and salt. Set aside. Mix sugar, margarine, and eggs. Beat well. Stir in bananas. Stir flour mixture into banana mixture just until smooth. Put in greased baking pan. Bake at 350° 50 to 60 minutes until firm when lightly touched at center. Let cool in pan 10 minutes.

Banana Cake No. 2

⅓ cup oil
2 ½ cups cake flour
1 teaspoon baking soda
1 teaspoon baking powder
1 teaspoon salt
1 ¼ cups fully ripe bananas, mashed
⅔ cup milk OR reconstituted nonfat dry milk
¾ tablespoon lemon juice (leave in milk for 5 minutes)
1 egg
1 teaspoon vanilla extract

Place oil in bowl. Sift in flour, sugar, soda, baking powder, and salt. Add bananas and ⅓ cup of milk/lemon juice mixture. Mix until moist. Beat 2 minutes at medium speed. Add remaining ⅓ cup milk/lemon juice mixture, egg, and vanilla and beat 2 minutes longer. Bake in 2 greased, round, and lightly floured 9 x 1 ½ inch pans at 350° about 35 minutes.

Banana Cake No. 3

1 cup flour
3 teaspoons baking powder
½ cup sugar
3 bananas, mashed
1 cup nonfat dry milk, reconstituted at 2X regular concentration
2 tablespoons oil

Sift dry ingredients together. Add milk and oil and mix well. Add bananas, and mix again. Pour in greased cake pan (8-inch), and bake at 375° for 1 hour or until toothpick comes out clean.

Banana-Oatmeal Cookies

1 ½ cups unsifted flour
1 cup sugar
½ teaspoon baking soda
1 teaspoon salt
¾ cup margarine
1 egg
2 cups bananas, mashed
1 ¾ cups uncooked quick rolled oats
½ cup raisins, if you like

Mix flour, sugar, baking soda, and salt in a large bowl. Mix in margarine with a fork or two knives until finely crumbled. Beat egg. Stir egg and rest of ingredients all at once into flour mixture. Beat well. Drop dough from a teaspoon on a greased baking pan. Bake at 400° about 12 minutes until browned.

Cheese Drop Biscuits

2 cups flour
1 tablespoon baking powder
½ teaspoon salt
⅓ cup oil
1 cup cut-up cheese (American or cheddar)
¾ cup fluid milk OR reconstituted nonfat dry milk at 2X concentration

Mix flour, baking powder, and salt in a large bowl. Mix in oil with a fork until mixture is crumbly. Stir in cheese and milk. Drop dough from tablespoon on greased baking pan. Bake at 450° (very hot oven) about 15 minutes until lightly browned.

Chocolate Cakes

2 cups flour

1 ¼ cups sugar
4 tablespoons powdered cocoa
1 teaspoon baking powder
½ teaspoon baking soda
¼ teaspoon salt
1 cup nonfat dry milk, reconstituted at 3X regular concentration
½ cup vegetable oil

Sift dry ingredients together. Add milk and mix well. Add oil and mix. Pour into 9 inch square pan and bake at 350° for 30 to 35 minutes. Cool and cut into 2 inch squares.

Chocolate Cornmeal Cookies

Use recipe for Cornmeal Cookies. Mix ¼ cup cocoa (dry powder) into cookie dough with rest of dry ingredients. Add ¼ cup fluid milk. Continue as for Cornmeal Cookies.

Coffee Flavored Cake

2 cups flour
1 cup sugar
2 teaspoons baking powder
½ cup nonfat dry milk, dissolved in ½ cup water
4 tablespoons instant coffee dissolved in ¼ cup hot water
1 egg, beaten
¼ cup oil

Sift dry ingredients together. Add egg, milk, coffee, and oil and mix well. Bake in greased square cake pan at 350° for 45 minutes or until done. Frost with a sweet frosting.

Cornbread or Muffins

1 cup cornmeal
1 cup unsifted flour
1 tablespoon baking powder
½ teaspoon salt
2 to 4 tablespoons sugar, if you like

1 egg
1 cup fluid milk
¼ cup oil

Mix cornmeal, flour, baking powder, salt and sugar (if used). Set aside.
Beat egg. Add milk. Add oil. Add to cornmeal mixture and stir just
enough to mix. Fill a greased pan half full. Bake at 425° 20 to 25
minutes until lightly browned. For muffins, fill greased muffin tins half
full of cornmeal mixture. Baking time will be 15 to 20 minutes.

Corn Grits Spoonbread

½ cup corn grits
1 cup uncooked cornmeal
2 teaspoons salt
3 tablespoons margarine
2 ½ cups water
2 cups nonfat dry milk, reconstituted at 2X regular concentration
2 eggs

Mix grits, cornmeal and salt. Add margarine. Stir in water and milk.
Cook and stir until mixture thickens a little. Beat eggs in a large bowl.
Stir cooked mixture slowly into eggs. Pour in greased baking pan. Bake
in 400° oven about 45 minutes until firm.

Cornmeal Cookies

¾ cup margarine
¾ cup sugar
1 egg
1 ½ cups flour
½ cup cornmeal
1 teaspoon baking powder
¼ teaspoon salt
1 teaspoon vanilla
½ cup raisins, if you like

Mix margarine and sugar in a large bowl. Add egg and beat well. Add
rest of ingredients and mix well. Drop dough from a teaspoon on a
greased baking pan. Bake at 350° about 15 minutes until lightly
browned.

Drop Biscuits

2 cups flour
1 tablespoon baking powder
1 teaspoon salt
⅓ cup oil
¾ cup fluid milk, or nonfat dry milk reconstituted at 2X regular concentration

Mix flour, baking powder, and salt. Mix in oil with a fork or two knives until crumbly. Add milk. Mix enough to wet dry ingredients. Drop dough from a tablespoon on greased baking pan. Bake at 450° 10 to 12 minutes until lightly browned.

Frosted Oatmeal Cookies

2 cups flour
½ teaspoon salt
2 teaspoons baking powder
½ teaspoon nutmeg
1 cup sugar
½ cup oil
1 egg
1 cup evaporated or condensed milk
1 ½ cups uncooked quick rolled oats
Vanilla Frosting (see recipe)

Mix flour, salt, baking powder, and nutmeg. Set aside. Mix sugar, oil, and egg. Beat well. Stir evaporated milk and rolled oats into sugar mixture. Mix in flour mixture. Drop dough from a teaspoon on a greased baking pan. Bake at 350° 18 to 20 minutes until lightly browned. Cool cookies and top with frosting.

Muffins

2 cups unsifted flour
1 tablespoon baking powder
¼ cup sugar
½ teaspoon salt
1 egg

1 cup fluid milk OR reconstituted nonfat dry milk at 2X regular concentration
¼ cup oil
½ cup raisins, if desired

Mix flour, baking powder, sugar, and salt. Set aside. Beat egg and add milk. Add oil. Add milk mixture and raisins to flour mixture. Stir until just mixed, leaving batter lumpy. Fill greased muffin tins half full. Bake at 400° 20 to 25 minutes until browned.

Oatmeal-Raisin Muffins

1 ¼ cups unsifted flour
1 tablespoon baking powder
1 teaspoon salt
⅓ cup sugar
1 cup uncooked quick rolled oats
½ cup raisins
1 egg
1 cup reconstituted nonfat dry milk at 2X regular concentration
⅓ cup oil

Mix flour, baking powder, salt, and sugar in a large bowl. Stir in rolled oats and raisins. Beat egg and add milk. Add oil. Set aside. Combine milk and flour mixtures. Stir just until dry ingredients are wet, leaving batter lumpy. Fill greased muffin pans half full. Bake at 400° 20 to 25 minutes until muffins are browned.

Peanut Butter and Oatmeal Cookies

1 cup margarine
2 cups sugar
¾ cups peanut butter
1 teaspoon vanilla
2 eggs
1 teaspoon baking soda dissolved in ½ teaspoon water
1 ⅓ cups flour
3 cups oatmeal

Mix first 3 ingredients. Add next 3 ingredients and mix well. Add last 2 ingredients and mix. Form balls about 1 inch in diameter, and flatten, if preferred. Bake at 350° for about 10 minutes. Makes about 4 dozen cookies. Immediately after removing them from the oven, place in tight container to keep them soft.

Peanut Butter Bread

1 ¾ cups unsifted flour
1 tablespoon baking powder
1 teaspoon salt
⅓ cup sugar
1 cup peanut butter
1 egg
1 ¼ cups nonfat dry milk, reconstituted at 2X regular concentration

Mix flour, baking powder, salt, and sugar in a large bowl. Mix in peanut butter with a fork until crumbly. Set aside. Beat egg slightly and add milk. Add milk mixture to flour mixture. Stir just enough to mix. Fill a greased loaf pan half full. Bake at 350° about 1 hour.

Peanut Butter Cake

2 cups unsifted flour
2 teaspoons baking powder
½ teaspoon baking soda
1 teaspoon salt
½ cup peanut butter
¼ cup margarine
1 ½ cups sugar
2 eggs
⅔ cup fluid milk, OR nonfat dry milk reconstituted at 2X regular concentration
1 teaspoon vanilla, if desired
Vanilla Cream Frosting (see recipe)

Mix flour, baking powder, baking soda, and salt. Set aside. Mix peanut butter, margarine and sugar in a large bowl until smooth. Add eggs and beat well. Add half of the flour mixture and half of the milk. Beat 200 times. Add rest of flour mixture and milk. Add vanilla. Fill a greased baking pan half full. Bake at 350° about 30 minutes until cake springs back when lightly touched near center. Frost with Vanilla Cream Frosting, if desired.

Peanut Butter Cookies No. 1

2 ½ cups flour
½ teaspoon salt
½ teaspoon baking soda
1 cup margarine
1 cup peanut butter
2 cups sugar
2 eggs

Mix flour, salt and baking soda. Set aside. Mix margarine and peanut butter. Add sugar. Mix well. Add eggs and beat well. Stir flour mixture into peanut butter mixture. Drop dough from a teaspoon onto greased cookie sheet. Flatten with a fork. Bake at 375° 10 to 15 minutes until lightly browned.

Peanut Butter Cookies No. 2

1 ½ cups white or whole wheat flour
1 cup sugar
½ cup peanut butter
¼ cup oil
¼ cup water

Mix ingredients into a dough. Roll out into thin sheet and cut into shapes or make small balls and flatten (fork indentation for design) and place on lightly greased (with oil) cookie sheet. Bake at 250° until edges are brown.

Pie Crust No. 1

2 cups sifted flour
1 teaspoon salt
½ cup oil
5 tablespoons very cold water

Sift flour and salt. Pour oil into cup and add water, but *do not stir*. Add oil/water to flour and mix with a fork until all flour is moistened. Shape into two balls. Wet counter, and put down large sheet of waxed paper and roll with rolling pin. Makes very flaky crust for top and bottom of 9 inch pie. Bake at 350° for one hour or according to specific pie instructions.

Pie Crust No. 2

2 cups flour
½ teaspoon salt
½ cup oil
5 tablespoons cold water
1 tablespoon sugar

Sift flour and salt and sugar. Add water to oil, but *do not stir*. Add to flour and mix until moist. Roll between two sheets of waxed paper. Makes double crust for 9 inch pie.

Pineapple Cake

2 cups flour
1 cup sugar
3 teaspoons baking powder
1 15 ¼-ounce can crushed pineapple
1 egg
½ cup oil

Sift dry ingredients. Add other ingredients, and mix well. Bake in greased square cake pan at 350° for 1 hour or until toothpick comes out clean.

Pineapple-Cottage Cheese Pie

2 cups creamed cottage cheese
1 egg
½ cup sugar
2 tablespoons flour
½ cup undrained, crushed pineapple
1 tablespoon lemon juice
Unbaked 8-inch single pie crust

Pineapple Glaze (recipe follows)

Mix cottage cheese and egg; beat well. Mix in sugar, flour, crushed pineapple and lemon juice. Pour into unbaked pie crust. Bake at 350° about 45 minutes until the tip of a knife stuck in the center comes out clean. Cool the pie. Spread Pineapple Glaze over top. Chill.

Pineapple Glaze

Mix ½ cup undrained crushed pineapple, 2 tablespoons lemon juice, and 1 tablespoon cornstarch in a pan. Cook and stir over low heat about 5 minutes until thickened and clear. Cool.

Quick Coffee Cake

2 cups flour
1 tablespoon baking powder
1 teaspoon salt
¾ cup sugar
½ cup margarine
1 egg
¾ cup reconstituted nonfat dry milk at 2X regular concentration
¼ cup raisins, if you like
¼ cup sugar
½ teaspoon cinnamon

Mix flour, baking powder, salt and ½ cup sugar. Mix in margarine with a fork or two knives until crumbly. Beat egg and add milk. Stir into flour mixture. Add raisins and mix well. Fill a greased baking pan half full. Mix ¼ cup sugar with cinnamon. Sprinkle over batter in pan. Bake at 400° 25 to 30 minutes until cake springs back when lightly touched near center.

Quick Raisin Bread

2 cups unsifted flour
4 teaspoons baking powder
½ teaspoon salt
1 teaspoon cinnamon, if desired

⅓ cup margarine
½ cup sugar
2 eggs
¾ cup dry nonfat milk, reconstituted at 2X regular concentration
1 cup raisins

Mix flour, baking powder, salt and cinnamon. Set aside. Mix margarine and sugar until smooth. Add eggs and beat well. Stir half the flour and half the milk into egg mixture. Stir in rest of flour and milk until dough is smooth. Stir in raisins. Pour in greased loaf pan. Bake at 350° about 40 minutes until browned. Cool bread in pan for 10 minutes.

Vanilla Cream Frosting

¼ cup margarine
2 cups confectioners sugar
3 tablespoons fluid milk (about)
1 teaspoon vanilla

Mix all ingredients, using 1 tablespoon of the milk. Mix in rest of milk, if needed, to make frosting that will spread easily but not run off cake.

Vanilla Frosting

1 ½ cups confectioners sugar
3 tablespoons evaporated milk
½ teaspoon vanilla

Stir all ingredients together until mixture is smooth. If frosting is too thick, add a few more drops of evaporated milk. If frosting is too thin, add a little more sugar.

SOUPS

Bean Chowder

1 cup dry pea (navy) beans or other dry white beans
4 cups water
1 teaspoon salt
2 medium-size carrots
1 small onion
1 can evaporated milk, or condensed milk (13 fluid ounces)
Salt and pepper to taste
Few drops hot pepper sauce, if desired

Wash and drain beans. Pressure cook beans and water for 45 to 60 minutes. Cut carrots in thin slices. Chop onion. Add to beans. Cover and cook until vegetables are tender.
Stir in evaporated milk. Heat, but do not boil.
Season to taste.

Bean Soup

1 ½ cups dry beans
7 cups water
1 medium-sized onion
1 teaspoon salt
Ham bone

Wash and drain beans.
Put beans and water in pan and bring to boiling. Boil 2 minutes. Remove from heat. Cover and let stand 1 hour. (You may pressure cook instead of boiling. Reduce time about one-third.)
Chop onion, add to beans.
Add salt and ham bone. Cover and boil gently 1 ½ to 2 ½ hours until beans are soft.
Add more water for thinner soup, if desired.

Cabbage Soup

Small head of green cabbage
1 lb. of beef bones, cut from steak or roast before cooking
1 medium onion
4 medium potatoes, peeled, but whole
1 one-pound can tomatoes
2 tablespoons lemon juice
1 tablespoon sugar, or to taste
Water
Salt to taste

Cut cabbage into chunks. Place in pot. Add all other ingredients. Cover completely with water. Boil for 1 ½ hours at low temperature.

Cream of Corn Soup

2 cups nonfat milk reconstituted at 2X regular concentration
1 teaspoon salt
2 tablespoons unsaturated oil
2 slices onion
1 can corn
2 tablespoons corn meal
2 tablespoons whole wheat OR rye flour

Put nonfat milk, salt, oil, and onion in pot and bring to simmering point. Add corn meal and corn. Simmer for 20 minutes. Gradually add flour, stir, and simmer for 10 minutes more or until mixture begins to thicken.

Enriched, Condensed Soups

1 can condensed soup
6 tablespoons soy OR rye flour
1 can water
Water to make thickening

Make smooth thickening of flour and water. Heat soup and the 1 can of water. Add thickening, and heat to serving temperature.

Suggested soups for this enrichment method are:
bean and bacon
green pea
cream of chicken
cream of celery
cream of mushroom
tomato

Lentil Soup

1 cup dried lentils
1 sliced onion
2 tablespoons oil
1 cup nonfat dry milk (reconstituted)
1 quart water
1 teaspoon thyme or parsley flakes
Salt to taste

Wash lentils and bring to boil in water. Meanwhile, heat oil and saute onion for 10 minutes. Drain off most of oil. Add to lentils and keep boiling over low heat for 45 minutes. Add milk, thyme, and salt and boil 10 minutes longer.
May also be cooked without the milk if desired.

Onion Soup, Iranian Style

3 medium onions, sliced thinly
3 tablespoons oil
2 tablespoons rye flour
3 cups water
1 teaspoon salt
½ teaspoon pepper
¼ teaspoon tumeric (if desired)
¼ teaspoon cinnamon
½ cup lemon juice
1 teaspoon sugar (about)

In large pot saute onions in oil. Add flour while stirring and cook for 5 minutes, making sure mixture is smooth. Add water and stir. Add salt, pepper, and tumeric. Cover and simmer for 30 minutes. Remove from heat, add cinnamon and lemon juice, and stir. Add sugar. Serve with pumpernickel or rye bread.

Split Pea Soup

1 large onion
3 tablespoons oil
1 ½ cups dry split peas
6 cups water
1 ½ teaspoons salt

Chop onion. Cook in oil in a large pan until tender.
Wash and drain split peas.
Add water, split peas, and salt to onion.
Bring to boiling. Lower heat and cover pan. Cook about 2 hours until thickened.

Note: Cook a ham bone in the soup if you like and reduce salt.

Split Pea Vegetable Soup

1 large potato
2 medium-sized carrots
2 stalks celery
½ small onion
½ cup dry split peas
1 ½ cup dry split peas
1 ½ quarts (6 cups) water
1 tablespoon oil
1 tablespoon salt and pepper if desired
¼ small head cabbage

Cut up potato, carrots, celery, and onion.
Wash and drain split peas.
Bring water to boiling. Add cut up vegetables, split peas, oil, salt, and pepper. Cover and boil gently 30 minutes.
Cut up cabbage and add to soup. Cook 15 minutes longer.

Vegetable Soup

4 stalks celery, with tops
1 medium-sized onion
2 medium-sized carrots
¼ small head cabbage
3 cups water
1 ½ cups cooked or canned tomatoes
¼ cup margarine
1 ½ teaspoons salt
Pepper, if desired
¼ cup uncooked rice

Cut up celery, onions, carrots, and cabbage.
Bring water to boiling and add all ingredients except rice. Cover and boil slowly 15 to 20 minutes, until vegetables are almost tender. Add rice.
Lower heat and cook about 25 minutes longer until rice is tender. Note: Add 3 beef bouillon cubes before cooking the soup, if you like. Other kinds of raw vegetables may be cooked in the soup. Cooked or canned vegetables may be added to the cooked soup.

DESSERTS

Barley Pudding

1 cup barley
3 cups water, ¼ teaspoon salt added
1 cup dried currants

Boil or pressure cook barley in salt water until soft. Drain excess water. Add currants, mix, and simmer for 30 minutes. Add more water as needed. Serve with a sweet sauce.

Bread Pudding

12 slices white bread

1 cup sugar
2 cups nonfat dry milk, reconstituted at 2x regular concentration
1 egg
Several drops vanilla extract
Salt to taste
1 tablespoon oil
2 tablespoons lemon juice

Dice bread. Add sugar to milk and stir until dissolved. Add egg, vanilla extract, salt, oil and lemon juice. Mix thoroughly. Add to bread, mixing into a pastry mess. Place in baking pan, and bake in moderate oven (350°) for 45 minutes. Serve with raisin sauce, prune sauce, fresh berries, or sliced fruit when cheap.

Cornmeal and Fruit Pudding

¾ cup cornmeal
4 tablespoons sugar plus 1 tablespoon for fruit
½ teaspoon salt
1 ½ cups nonfat dry milk
¼ cup prunes, pitted and diced
¼ cup seedless raisins
¼ cup apricots, diced
¼ cup red currants
1 ¾ cups water
1 tablespoon oil

Cook cornmeal, sugar, salt, and milk until mushy. Also, in water cook prunes, raisins, apricots, and currants and 1 tablespoon of sugar in water until soft. When cornmeal has a mushy consistency, fold in the fruit, stirring carefully. Add the oil while stirring. Place in baking dish and bake for 20 minutes at 350°. Serve warm.

Dutch Apple Pudding

1 ½ cups sifted flour
½ teaspoon salt
2 teaspoons baking powder
1 cup nonfat dry milk, reconstituted at 2X regular concentration
2 tablespoons oil

¾ cup sugar
3 cups apples, peeled and sliced
Cinnamon to taste

Make a batter of flour, salt, baking powder, milk, oil, and sugar. Mix in 2 cups of apples. Pour in baking dish, and place remaining cup of apples on top, sprinkle with cinnamon and sugar, and dot with margarine. Bake at 350° for 50 minutes.

Enriched Canned Fruit

1 can canned fruit (fruit cocktail is good)
¼ cup nonfat dry milk (in powder form)
3 tablespoons sugar
5 drops vanilla extract
Liquid from fruit

Carefully pour off liquid from fruit into mixing bowl. Add nonfat dry milk, sugar and vanilla extract and beat at high speed with electric mixer until very smooth. Add fruit and mix gently until fruit is well blended with sauce.

Grapefruit Candy

4 grapefruit skins (after grapefruit is eaten)
1 ¼ lbs. sugar
1 lemon

Remove outer rind from grapefruit skins with a fine knife. Discard outer rind and use only the inner white pectin. Cut into eighths. Wash in cold water and drain. Put in pot and cover with cold water. Boil for 10 minutes. Discard the boiled water. Add more cold water and boil again. Discard boiled water again (this removes bitter taste). Drain thoroughly. Replace in pot. Add the sugar. Peel outer rind from lemon and discard rind. Cut lemon into 6 slices. Add lemon to pot. Don't add any water. Stir thoroughly. Put on low heat and keep it there for about 2 hours, stirring frequently. When all liquid is cooked out of peel, remove from stove. Place each piece separately on wax paper and allow to dry overnight. May be stored indefinitely if kept dry.

Instant Banana Ice Milk No. 1

1 cup nonfat dry milk powder (dry)
¾ cup sugar
1 teaspoon vanilla flavoring
4 bananas, mashed
2 cups water

Mix ingredients together and place in freezing compartment. Serve when thick and cold.

Instant Banana Ice Milk No. 2

1 cup nonfat dry milk, reconstituted
½ cup sugar
1 teaspoon vanilla
1 egg
2 bananas, mashed

Mix all ingredients in blender. Chill until very cold.

Orange-Raisin Rice

½ cup sugar
⅓ cup water
2 cups rice, cooked
½ cup raisins
1 tablespoon margarine
1 cup orange juice
½ cup chopped peanuts, if desired

Heat water and sugar in heavy pan until warm. Add rice, raisins and margarine. Cook over medium heat 5 minutes. Stir in orange juice. Serve warm or cold. Sprinkle with chopped peanuts.

Peanut Butter Pudding No. 1

2 tablespoons cornstarch
¼ cup sugar

½ teaspoon salt
¼ cup peanut butter
1 egg
2 cups nonfat dry milk, reconstituted at 2X regular concentration
1 teaspoon vanilla

Mix cornstarch, sugar, and salt in a pan. Add peanut butter and mix until crumbly. Beat egg. Put egg and milk in the pan. Cook and stir over medium heat until mixture thickens. Cook and stir 1 minute longer. Stir in vanilla. Chill before serving.

Peanut Butter Pudding No. 2

1 cup oatmeal
1 cup water
1 cup nonfat dry milk, reconstituted at 2X regular concentration
4 tablespoons peanut butter
4 tablespoons sugar
¼ teaspoon salt
½ tablespoon oil

Cook oatmeal with water and milk until it reaches consistency of cream. Stir in sugar and peanut butter until thoroughly dissolved. Place oil in baking dish, and add pudding. Bake at 350° for 30 minutes. Serve with a sweet, or a sweet-sour sauce.

Raisin-Rice Pudding

2 cups water
½ cup uncooked rice
½ teaspoon salt
⅓ cup raisins
1 tablespoon margarine
1 cup nonfat dry milk (not instant) or 2 cups instant nonfat dry milk (as powder)
½ cup sugar
1 cup warm water
1 teaspoon vanilla

Heat 2 cups water to boiling. Stir in rice, salt, raisins, and margarine.

Lower heat, cover, and cook 30 minutes. Remove from heat. Mix dry milk and sugar. Mix in 1 cup warm water until smooth. Add milk mixture and vanilla to rice. Stir over low heat until hot. Cool to thicken.

Vanilla Cream Pudding or Pie

2 tablespoons cornstarch
¼ cup sugar
¼ teaspoon salt
1 egg
2 cups nonfat dry milk, reconstituted at 2X regular concentration
1 tablespoon margarine
1 teaspoon vanilla

Mix cornstarch, sugar, and salt in pan. Set aside. Beat egg and add milk. Stir into cornstarch mixture. Cook and stir over medium heat until mixture thickens. Cook and stir 1 minute longer. Stir in margarine and vanilla. Chill before serving. For vanilla cream pie, use 3 tablespoons cornstarch in place of 2. Pour cooled pudding into a baked pie crust. Put fresh or canned fruit on the pie, if you like.

SAUCES AND SYRUPS

Cinnamon Cream Pancake Syrup

1 cup corn syrup
2 cups sugar
½ cup water
2 teaspoons cinnamon
1 cup evaporated or condensed milk

Put all ingredients except evaporated or condensed milk in a large saucepan. Heat to boiling, stirring all the time. Cook and stir 2 minutes longer. Cool 5 minutes. Stir in evaporated milk. Serve warm or cold. Store unused syrup in refrigerator.

Fruit Sauce

2 to 4 tablespoons sugar
2 tablespoons cornstarch
2 cups liquid from canned fruits
1 tablespoon lemon juice
1 cup crushed, drained, canned fruit

Mix sugar and cornstarch in pan. Stir in fruit liquid. Cook and stir until thickened. Stir in lemon juice and crushed fruit.
Serve hot or cold on pancakes, plain cake, ice cream, custard or pudding.

Orange or Lemon Sauce

Frozen orange juice or lemon juice, undiluted, makes an excellent flavoring sauce for broiled chicken and other dishes.

Prune Sauce

⅓ pound dried prunes
⅔ cup nonfat dry milk, reconstituted at 2X regular concentration
1 cup water

Remove prune pits and cut or chop prunes into small pieces. Simmer in water until prunes are quite soft, and water is brownish—approximately 30 minutes. Add nonfat milk, bring back to simmering point, remove from stove and cool. Mix in blender. Serve over cheese, fish, or fruit dishes, or puddings. For desserts, add one tablespoon sugar.

Raisin Syrup

1 cup sugar
2 tablespoons cornstarch
¼ teaspoon cinnamon
½ cup corn syrup
1 cup water
¼ cup margarine
1 cup raisins

Mix all ingredients except raisins in a pan. Bring to boiling. Lower heat. Cook and stir 6 or 7 minutes until thickened. Stir in raisins. Serve over pancakes or French toast.

White Sauce (Medium-Thick)

2 tablespoons margarine
2 tablespoons flour (rye or white)
¼ teaspoon salt
1 cup nonfat dry milk, reconstituted at 2X regular concentration

Melt margarine in a pan. Stir in flour and salt. Slowly stir in milk to make a smooth mixture. Cook and stir over medium heat until mixture comes to boiling. Lower heat. Cook and stir about 3 minutes until thickened.

Chapter 6

THE POLITICS OF FOOD

HOW FOOD COST INFLATION AFFECTS YOU, HOW IT DEVELOPED, AND WHAT SHOULD BE DONE ABOUT IT ON A NATIONAL LEVEL

The average American may not be aware, when the total weekly cost of food for a family rises by $10, that he is actually losing much more than that amount. The prices of goods other than food (hardware, clothing, automobiles) and services (dentist, carpenter, hairdresser) are also rising, because those involved in delivering those goods and services must have more money to meet their own food budgets.

There are other less obvious losses, and one of them is a decrease in the true value of your social security account. The amount of money in the account does not drop, but its purchasing power does. Some lose more, and some less. The more money in the account, the more is lost. A reasonable estimate is that on the average, about $5 per week in true value is lost when the price of food rises by $10 per week.

Ironically, the average American family also lost about $1 per week until 1974, which the Federal Government took out of their taxes to pay people *not* to raise food. This dollar was not your total contribution to the Department of Agriculture, it was only the cost of the program that paid the owners of farmland over $2 *billion* in 1972 to keep their land out of production. We will have more to say about this incredible situation later, but it is pertinent

144

to point out here that the small family farmer was not the beneficiary of this program.

Finally, even if you manage to increase your income to compensate for the increased price of food, you lose again because of the graduated income tax system. This kind of loss is somewhat complex, but a simple example may explain its effect, even if the mechanism does not seem to make sense. Let us assume that the total net taxable income of an American family after all deductions and exemptions is $12,000. The current tax is $1,380, leaving a net living allowance of $10,620. Let us suppose that the cost of living goes up 10 percent, and that salaries and income also go up 10 percent. Now the total net taxable income of this family is $12,000 + $1,200 or $13,200. The income tax on this is $1,680, leaving a net living allowance of $11,520. At first, this might seem an improvement over the original net living allowance of $10,620, but we must remember that prices have risen by 10 percent. Therefore, the $11,520 is only worth 90 percent of what it appears to be, or $10,368 in the former dollars. The difference between $10,620 and $10,368 is $252, which is the loss due to the combined effects of graduated income tax and inflation. *In other words, even if gross income goes up just as much as prices, the net true purchasing power will fall.* It is difficult to estimate how this effect can be translated into dollars per week for an average family since incomes differ, but the loss is significant.

When we total up these losses, it becomes clear that a $10 per week increase in the price of food for a family is likely to mean a true financial loss of about $30 per week. The squeeze affects not only the individual family, but also is having long-range deleterious effects on institutions which affect us all, such as hospitals and schools. For example, when an institution such as a cancer hospital and research center must allow for substantial increases in its food budget, the research area suffers because of cut-backs in funding.

Clearly, the situation is much more serious than one might gather from the raw statistics released by the government. It is correspondingly more important to solve this problem. There are both long-term and short-term causes for the rise in food prices, and there are long-term and short-term actions which will help

reverse the trend. Both must be used, or any improvement will
be only temporary.

HOW DID THE INFLATION IN
FOOD PRICES DEVELOP?

Several factors have contributed to the inflation in food prices.
One is the growth in population. Another is the increase in
demand for certain foods such as meat. These factors, however,
only account for a relatively small part of the inflation. The
major causes of food price inflation seem to be in certain
government programs and in the lack of other programs.

For decades now we have had a series of government farm
programs superimposed upon each other. The announced purpose
of these programs has been entirely praiseworthy—to enable the
farmer to make a reasonable living. Each farmer now has to
provide food for about 40 other Americans, and there is no doubt
that he deserves a fair break. Most farmers in the past and many
today work long hours and receive little in return. They have to
contend with floods, droughts, windstorms, brush fires, plant
diseases, fluctuations in prices, and other problems. In principle,
government assurance to a farmer that if he works hard and
efficiently, he can keep his farm and make a decent living is
completely proper. The United States Government provides
similar assurances for many persons and industries in effect,
although they may not be formalized into law. If there were good
evidence that the current inflation in food prices were needed to
provide fair treatment for American farmers, one might well
decide that the inflation is not too high a price for such a
worthwhile goal. The question, then, is whether the government
policies have in fact been providing reasonable security for
farmers and giving them a fair break. The answer appears to be
clearly negative. An article in "Science," May 18, 1973, points
out that since 1940 when these farm programs really became big,
over 30 *million* farm residents have left their farms for the cities.
Even now, 800,000 people leave the farm *each year* to move to
cities. Each *week,* 2,000 farms go out of business. Poverty is
common among farm families. This is not due to laziness or

inefficiency. It is due to confused, outmoded government programs.

By 1967, American farmers were able to produce on one acre of land in one year enough basic foods to keep a working man strong and healthy for over four *years*. By basic foods, I refer to grains, beans, peanuts, potatoes, and some vegetables. Although not up to present American standards of variety, this would provide a better diet than that eaten by 90 percent of the world's population. Since 1967, the American farmer has done even better.

The present inflation in food prices has not solved the farmer's problem, and the aftermath may make his situation much worse. Money is certainly being made out of high food prices, but the farmer isn't making it. For example, Russia recently bought several *million tons* of grain from America. The American taxpayers paid hundreds of millions of dollars in subsidies to those who sold the grain to Russia. However, the sellers were not farmers! They were wheat speculators. Farmers received about 2 ½ *cents* per pound for their wheat. (This doesn't leave much margin for profit.) The grain speculators bought the wheat, negotiated the deal with Russia with the help of the United States Government, and collected money from Russia as well as from the United States Government as subsidies. The whole deal was shrouded in secrecy, and no one seems to know how much profit the speculators made, but it must have been a lot.

The United States Congress has shown some annoyance with this deal that bilked the farmers, increased food prices, and cost the taxpayers hundreds of millions of dollars. One senator implied that an assistant secretary of agriculture had behaved improperly. The official he referred to arranged the negotiations with the Russians and then resigned to become an officer in a company that sold *four million tons* of wheat to Russia and collected the largest subsidies. In defense of his own position, the official's superior, Secretary of Agriculture Butz, publicly stated that he had *no knowledge* that the Russians were buying millions of tons of American grain. Let's assume this is true. What kind of an agriculture department do we have if the man in charge doesn't know that millions of tons of grain are being sold to

Russia? The most charitable interpretation one can place on these events is that the Agriculture Department needs revision.

Let us now consider a few specific government agriculture programs that have contributed to the present situation. First, there are the so-called "Agriculture Stabilization and Conservation Programs" that pay the owners of farmland *not* to grow crops. Between 1971 and 1972, this program was increased by over 85 percent. In 1972, over 45 *million* acres of good farmland were kept out of production. This is approximately the total amount of farmland in all of France. In order to accomplish this, the federal government spent over $2 *billion* in taxpayers' money in 1972. Keeping that land out of production reduced our crops, reduced feed for cattle, hogs and poultry, and played a major role in raising the cost of food. Some of the money spent to keep the land out of production went to farmers, and some didn't. The exact proportions are not known. The entitlement to this government subsidy goes with the ownership of the land. If a farmer sells land that has some set-aside acreage, the new owner continues to collect the government payments even if he isn't a farmer and doesn't live near a farm. How and why did this program arise? In theory, it had two worthwhile purposes. First it was supposed to increase farm income so farmers would get a fair break. It has been in existence some twenty years in various guises, and during that period farmers have been forced off their farms in enormous numbers, as pointed out earlier. Clearly this program has not helped farmers. A second major purpose was supposed to be land conservation. In theory, leaving the land fallow would increase its productivity in later years. This theory was perfectly sound until about 30 years ago. In modern farming, however, if enough fertilizer is added to the soil, it is unnecessary to leave the land fallow, and this practice is now obsolete. Indeed, agriculture officials are well aware of this. There is no legal requirement that the set-aside land be rotated. An owner of farmland can leave the same parcel of ground fallow year after year, and he will still collect the full payment.

A second major way in which unwise government policies have worsened the situation is by the depletion and virtual wipe-out of our emergency food reserve. This has already had undesirable effects on food prices, but the most serious effect has, luckily, not yet come to pass. For many years, the United States had an emergency stockpile of staple foods enough to provide for the people for two years. We will consider the emergency insurance aspects of this program later. First, though, we may consider its relationship to the current inflation in food prices. As long as the government held a large supply of food and feed staples, there was a dampening effect on speculation in grains and soybeans. If prices became too high, the government could sell some of its stocks and bring prices down. As soon as the stocks were gone, however, this dampening effect disappeared, and speculators drove some prices sky high. Indeed, speculation in soybean futures had to be stopped by the exchanges (private organizations of speculators) because there were already signed contracts for more soybeans than the total national crop. When the speculators cornered the market, they were then able to raise soybean prices to several times their usual price. The situation will almost certainly worsen during the next year, and it would not be surprising if the soybean speculators get prices of three to five times the usual soybean prices. In a belated attempt to correct this situation, the United States Government temporarily banned exports of soybeans to Japan. This was one blunder added to another. The Japanese are our allies, and for years their people have depended on American soybeans as their main source of protein, and they paid a fair price for it. The Japanese are now seeking another source of soybeans, and when they find it—probably by contracting with another nation to produce them—a major market for United States soybeans will be jeopardized or lost. The psychological effect on our allies is another harmful result.

WHAT SHOULD BE DONE AT THE NATIONAL LEVEL

The inflation in food prices was caused largely by unwise federal policies and it can be corrected only by changing those policies. Consumer actions can help, but the main remedy must come from Washington, and this can happen only if consumers act in their capacity as voters and insist on more sensible policies.

There is no intent here to engage in partisan politics. We are not concerned with determining whether Congress or the President, the Republicans or the Democrats are primarily at fault. Our concern is to correct what is wrong promptly and efficiently. The first step is to understand which government policies are inflationary and which are not.

Sometimes there is a tendency to lump all government expenditures as inflationary, but this is completely incorrect. Whether or not an expenditure is inflationary depends not on its size, but on what it is spent for and what it achieves. This distinction is absolutely vital. Without it, there is a real danger that unwise actions would curtail the anti-inflationary programs as well as the inflationary ones and make the situation much worse. The solution to the inflation in food prices cannot be found in blindly cutting federal programs and expenditures. Instead, careful analysis is needed to determine which programs are truly inflationary. In general, government programs may be divided into three main groups: inflationary, noninflationary, and anti-inflationary.

Inflationary programs are those which result in higher prices without any equivalent increase in value received. The best example of an inflationary program has already been discussed—the payment to landowners not to grow crops. In 1972, this $2 billion dollar program gave little or no value to the taxpayers, and caused a shortage of some types of food with rising prices. A second example of an inflationary program is the export subsidy program for foods.

Examples of noninflationary programs are: publishing by the United States Government Printing Office (the largest publisher in the world); regulatory programs, such as the Fair Trade Commission, law enforcement activities, and civil defense. Such programs have little if any effect on inflation one way or the other.

Anti-inflationary programs are those which result in a profit for the government, or lower prices for the consumer, or significant benefits for the public that outweigh the costs, or a combination of these. The best example of an anti-inflationary program is the Tennessee Valley Authority (T.V.A.). The T.V.A. is paying the federal treasury back, with interest, all the money that was appropriated to put it in operation. Thus, the federal government will make a profit. The T.V.A., by promoting efficiency, has markedly lowered the price of electricity to consumers in a multi-state area. The T.V.A. has developed new fertilizers which enable farmers all over the nation to produce more crops at a lower cost. In addition, the T.V.A. has provided many other benefits, not only to the people of its area, but to Americans throughout the nation.

A second type of anti-inflationary expenditure is support of medical research. A study has shown that between 1944 and 1967, medical research findings saved approximately 8 million American lives.* Most of these were children or adults in their productive years. The wage earners in this group paid to the federal government $12.8 billion in income and excise taxes during the 23-year period, a greater amount than the government had invested in medical research! Furthermore, this figure does not include the taxes paid after 1967, lives saved after 1967 by discoveries made previously, or the amount added to national income and federal tax receipts by wage earners who were spared long periods of disability and loss of work by medical research discoveries. When studies are done on a particular year, the same pattern emerges. For example, in 1967 the federal government invested $1.5 billion in medical research. In that same year, the wage earners spared from death by earlier medical research discoveries paid the federal government $1.7 billion in income and excise taxes. Therefore, the government made a substantial profit on its investment, again not counting its additional profit on taxes paid by those who were spared crippling and chronic disease. Studies are now planned to see what happened in subsequent years. Preliminary estimates show an even greater profit margin for the government. Of course, this is only one aspect of the benefits of government support of medical research. Other human benefits are more important, but less easy to measure. One measurement, however, is clear and striking. Between 1943 and 1967, medical research discoveries supported by the federal government added seven years to the life

---

*"Does Medical Research Pay Off in Lives? In Dollars?" New York: National Health Education Committee, Inc., 1970.

expectancy of each American. This was done at a yearly cost that never even reached $10 per American!

Perhaps the most important discovery in this area cannot be given a monetary value. It is the development of an effective oral contraceptive. This development now gives mankind the opportunity to avoid recurrent cycles of overpopulation and the resulting famine and disease.

Another anti-inflationary program is disaster prevention. Flood control dams, farm ponds, and wind-break tree plantings are programs that have paid excellent dividends in terms of saving both crops and human lives. Systems to provide warning of other disasters such as hurricanes and tornadoes, and the encouragement of measures that would minimize damage and loss when such disasters occur also help prevent inflation as well as help people. Programs to aid in recovery from disasters that could not be prevented also help prevent inflation. An important feature of disaster recovery is the availability of plentiful stocks of food in the event that our agricultural production is seriously damaged. We will return to this point again.

Clearly, solutions are not to be found in across-the-board cuts in federal programs either generally or even in a single department. The Department of Agriculture is supporting programs that are inflationary, non-inflationary, and anti-inflationary, and specific elimination or curtailment of the inflationary programs is what is needed. How is this to be approached? Some corrections can be made now. Others will require careful study.

One of the corrections that should be made at once is a standardization of measuring units. The Department of Agriculture pays subsidies and buys commodities on the basis of a variety of measuring units, and it is therefore quite difficult for the average person to make meaningful comparisons. Some foods are measured in pounds, others in hundredweights, others at times in tons, and still others in bushels. To add to the confusion, a bushel of one commodity does not weigh the same as a bushel of another commodity. As a result it is hard to judge whether a particular price floor is reasonable or not. Accordingly, all agriculture programs should be based on the same unit of measurement—pounds. A simple example of the value of this change would be its significance to the housewife when the price of bread goes up. Right now, when she hears that wheat has gone up from a certain amount per bushel to a larger amount, she cannot readily assess the fairness of a subsequent rise in the cost of bread. Few housewives know how much a bushel of wheat weighs (60 pounds). On the other hand, if the price of wheat goes from 6 cents per pound to 6½ cents per pound, the housewife (and the Congress) can readily see that a rise in the cost of bread from 28 cents per pound to 38 cents per pound is not justified. Furthermore, when American citizens realize that the farmer is only getting 3 to 6 cents per pound for his shelled grain, they will realize that he deserves an assurance that prices will not go lower. Also, they will realize that stockpiling grain at a purchase price of 6 to 8 cents per pound is not extravagant on the part of the government.

Two programs should be discontinued entirely. One is the so-called set-aside program for farm lands, which was discussed earlier. Around the middle of 1973, this program was temporarily waived, but payments apparently continued. It is quite possible for the program to be reinstated, with subsequent shortages and inflationary crises unless it is eliminated by revision of the law.

The export subsidy is another practice that should be eliminated. This program not only precipitated an acute inflation in food prices; it short-changed the farmer and cost the taxpayer hundreds of millions of dollars. If a particular nation cannot afford to pay the regular price of our product, it may be a good idea for our government to help them. However, this can be done openly and directly, without paying hundreds of millions of taxpayer money to food speculators.

All exporting of basic grains and soybeans should be taken out of the hands of the speculators and handled directly by the United States Government. This suggestion will be vigorously resisted by the speculators who have made fortunes by exporting, but it is a vital step. At this time, it is quite possible and legal for food speculators to ship practically all of our basic crops to other nations. By so doing, they might make more millions, but the American people would face not only a terrible inflation, but actual hunger. To some, this possibility might seem remote, but how many people two or three years ago foresaw the present

enormous rise in food costs? It might be argued that a serious
food shortage in this country would not occur, since the
government, on an emergency basis, could embargo food
shipments. This is a possibility, but it raises as many problems as
it solves. Suppose in the future, Russia, acting in good faith, has
signed a contract with food exporters for a large part of the
American crop. Suppose that the American government then
steps in and prevents the contract from being carried out. What
kind of international crisis might that precipitate? It would be far
better if the United States Government controlled all food exports
directly. Naturally, the suggestion that we continue a normal
trade relationship with Russia presupposes that Russia does not
become involved in active hostilities against a nation friendly to
the United States.

One program that was mistakenly eliminated should be
reinstated at once. That is the purchase and storage of basic
foods. This program was originally started as an aid to the
farmer, but actually it is of even more value to the consumer. At
the economic level this program can prevent wild jumps in the
price of foods. Perhaps more important is its value as an
insurance policy against food shortages and even starvation
caused by a disaster.

Americans have become so accustomed to plenty that they
seldom consider the possibility of a sudden food shortage, but in
the history of mankind, more than one flourishing civilization has
vanished because of a drastic reduction in food supply. Despite
our size, our prosperity, and our diversity, we are not immune to
famine, and there are several ways in which our food supply
might suddenly be reduced. Many fungi parasitize food crops,
and most of the time the skillful use of resistant strains of plants
and fungicides can minimize or eliminate their effects. Fungi,
however, are evolving life forms which usually multiply much
more rapidly than food plants, and consequently, they can also
mutate more rapidly. Mutant forms of fungi could attack plants
which are resistant to the old fungal strains and cause major crop
failures. The disastrous potato famine in Ireland occurred through
such a mechanism. Fungi also develop resistance to chemical
fungicides in the same way that bacteria develop resistance to
antibiotics. Epidemics of mutant fungi could destroy most of our
food crops or poison the food as ergot sometimes poisons rye.

A thermonuclear war would eliminate at least one year's crop, and probably more because of the effects of radioactive fallout.

Sudden changes in the climate might also be disastrous. Our major crops still depend on rainfall, and we could probably survive one year of severe, widespread drought. After that, we would face starvation.

If our ability to produce adequate food were severely curtailed by these or any other mechanisms, we might be able to buy minimal amounts of food from other nations, but not enough to keep us going for long. After all, the two biggest nations in the world, Russia and China, are themselves short of food and buying from us.

A few years ago, our granaries held a two-year supply of basic grains and beans. Today, we have only enough for a month or two, excluding stocks in stores and commercial warehouses. We need a basic food reserve that is large enough to support our people until farmers can restore our agriculture after a major catastrophe. How large a supply of stored food would that be? No one can predict. The Bible offers some guidance. Joseph saved Egypt by persuading the Pharaoh to store a seven-year supply of grain. The wisdom of Joseph is a good model to follow, but it might be difficult to implement. Certainly, a two-year supply of food should be considered a minimal goal. A basic daily ration of 1½ pounds per person should be stored. This would cost about 9 cents per person per day. Fortunately, most of the basic grains and dried beans remain edible for decades and even centuries when properly stored. Rotation with fresh crops virtually eliminates most losses.

One objection raised to such food storage is that in the past storage costs ran as high as $300 million per year. That is certainly a substantial sum. However, as an insurance policy for over 200 million Americans, it is rather inexpensive—about $1.50 per person per year for the storage. Not only would the stored food be an insurance against starvation, it would also be a deterrent to wild price fluctuations in food prices. The price of the food itself should be thought of as a saving until the grain is consumed, just as money or precious metal stored in a vault is a saving rather than an expenditure. It is a bit difficult to understand why some government officials should object to paying $300 million per year in food storage costs when they apparently did not object to paying $300 million in a few months to food speculators in export subsidies.

Prices for the food to be stored should be set at a level that will be fair to both the farmer and the taxpayer, and there should be a set maximum limit on the amount that any farmer can receive per year. These prices are for the grain or bean itself; for example, they would apply to kernels of corn, not to corn on the cob. A reasonable limit any farmer would receive per year from government sales would be $20,000. This would be a gross maximum payment, not to be confused with income or wages, since there are many out-of-pocket costs sustained by the farmer. Probably no more than $5,000 would be the equivalent of income, which is not excessive, and when added to other farm income should make it possible for farmers to keep their farms.

From time to time, the government could, by giving 12 months' notice, change the relative prices or stipulate certain proportions in the foods it will buy in order to maintain a balanced food reserve.

Carefully drawn and scrupulously enforced rules and regulations should prevent any evasion of the legal maximum payment on the part of the farmer, such as dividing farms among family members, phony land transfers, and so forth. Payment should be made directly to, and only to, the producer, not to any secondary purchaser. Most farmers will grow more than they sell to the government. The remainder would be sold on the open market, probably at lower prices, or used as feed for livestock, or exported.

Insuring a supply of meat both at reasonable prices and adequate to the demand in this country is a difficult task, because beef production cannot be increased as rapidly as can grain production. The elimination of hold-back provisions (paying landowners not to grow crops) and export subsidies and the provision of a food reserve should eventually help stabilize meat prices. It may or may not be advisable to institute some sort of long-term guarantee of meat prices to insure a steady supply. However, over the short term (2 years or so) there is no chance of keeping meat prices at a reasonable level by any or all of these measures, since each mature cow can produce only one calf per year, and therefore the number of new cattle in any given year cannot rise above a certain level; although it can go down, due to deaths on the range. The situation is similar with sheep, and somewhat different with hogs. Consequently, the maximum number of meat animals for next year is already relatively fixed, and two years from now will only be slightly larger. Meanwhile, consumer demand for meat will remain high, and unless something is done, meat prices will either go sky high—to $3 and $4 per pound—or meat may become unobtainable. Since we cannot do much to increase the number of meat animals in a short time, what can be done? One possibility would be to increase the amount of meat obtained from each animal by holding animals until they have reached a higher weight.

Of course, the shortage of meat may prove a blessing in disguise. A major cause of death—heart attacks—is probably due to excess intake of saturated fats, and meat is a major source of saturated fat. Perhaps during the forthcoming meat shortage, the death rate from heart attacks will drop, a phenomenon which did occur in Denmark during World War II when meats and other foods high in saturated fats became scarce. We may be forced to change our dietary habits, obtaining vital protein from sources other than meat. The suggested meat-extender dishes in this book are given with this eventuality in mind.

A complete revision of our agriculture program is long overdue. The total program is a helter-skelter conglomeration of separate projects, some which overlap, and some of which conflict with each other. A carefully thought out revision is needed, not only to deal fairly with farmers, but also to insure others a secure food supply. The situation is complex, and not readily handled by the usual governmental procedures. I suggest the appointment by the Congress of a National Panel of Consultants on Agriculture. Such a panel, composed of experts in the relevant areas, could investigate the situation and develop a comprehensive, effective plan to put our agriculture in order.

FOODS AND THEIR
FAIR-VALUE RANGES

The listing of foods and their fair-value ranges that begins on the next page is a shortened version of the Food Value Counter on pages 30-67 of this book. In this abbreviated form, only column 7, the total value range per pound expressed in cents per pound, is given for each food. An explanation of the chart and how to use it may be found on pages 23-29. For easy reference at the supermarket, the following pages may be cut from the book.

Food	Range
almonds, dried	
in shell	37-46
shelled	74-93
anchovy	75-94
apples	
dried, sulfured	29-36
fresh, good quality	13-16
frozen, sweetened	15-19
apple butter	25-31
apple juice, canned or bottled	8-10
applesauce, canned	
sweetened	13-16
unsweetened	11-14
apricots	
canned, light sirup pack	22-28
dried, sulfured	41-51
frozen, sweetened	18-23
raw	18-23
apricot nectar, canned	12-15
asparagus	
canned, spears, green	19-24
frozen, cuts and tips	16-20
raw, spears	13-16
avocados, raw, all commercial varieties	19-24
bacon	
Canadian, unheated	73-91
cured, sliced, raw	34-43
bananas, raw, good quality	15-19
barley, pearled, light	47-59
bass	
smallmouth and largemouth, raw, whole	20-25
striped, raw, whole	28-35
beans, common, mature seeds, dry	
white	
canned	
with pork and sweet sauce	23-29
with pork and tomato sauce	22-28
without pork	22-28
raw	51-64
red	
canned, with solids and liquid	19-24
raw	52-65
pinto, calico, red Mexican, raw	53-66
other, including black, brown, and Bayo, raw	51-64
beans, lima	
canned, regular pack	21-26
frozen	
baby limas	25-31
Fordhooks	23-29
immature seeds, raw	
in pod	13-16
shelled	28-35
mature seeds, dry, raw	49-61
beans, snap	
green	
canned, regular pack	12-15

Food	Range
frozen, cut	14-18
raw	14-18
yellow, or wax, raw	14-18
beans and frankfurters, canned	36-45
beef	
chuck cuts, choice grade	
arm	
with bone	65-81
without bone	72-90
entire chuck	60-75
with bone	60-75
without bone	74-93
rib, 5th	54-68
with bone	54-68
without bone	62-78
flank steak, choice grade	77-96
hamburger, raw	
lean	76-95
regular	67-84
hindshank, choice grade	
with bone	37-46
without bone	68-85
loin or short loin, choice gr.	
club steak	51-64
porterhouse steak	53-66
T-bone steak	51-64
loin end or sirloin, choice gr.	
double-bone sirloin steak	
with bone	53-66
without bone	62-78
hipbone sirloin steak	
with bone	49-61
without bone	56-70
wedge and round-bone sirloin	
with bone	60-75
without bone	64-80
rib, choice grade	
entire rib, 6-12th ribs	
with bone	53-66
without bone	57-71
rib, 6th or blade	
with bone	57-71
without bone	61-76
ribs, 11th-12th	
with bone	50-63
without bone	54-68
round, entire, choice grade	
with bone	72-90
without bone	74-93
rump, choice grade	
with bone	57-71
without bone	65-81
short plate, choice grade	
with bone	52-65
without bone	57-71
beef and vegetable stew, canned	32-40
beef, roast, canned	95-119
beef, corned, boneless	
canned, medium-fat	96-120
uncooked, medium-fat	60-75
beef, dried, chipped	23-154
beef potpie, frozen	39-49
beets, common, red	
canned, regular pack	16-20
raw, without tops	11-14

Food	Range
beet greens, common, raw	13-16
biscuits, baking powder, made from home-style recipe with enriched flour	41-51
biscuit dough, with enriched flour, frozen	32-40
biscuit mix, enriched flour, dry form	37-46
blackberries, including dewberries, boysenberries, youngberries, raw	18-23
blackberries, canned, heavy sirup	18-23
blackberry juice, canned, unsweetened	10-13
blueberries	
frozen, unsweetened	14-18
raw	14-18
bluefish, raw, whole	39-49
Boston brown bread	32-40
brains, all kinds, raw	0
bran, added sugar and malt extract	52-65
bran flakes	
40% bran	49-61
with raisins	46-58
brazilnuts	
in shell	30-38
shelled	63-79
bread	
cracked wheat	43-54
French or Vienna, enriched flour	45-56
Italian, enriched flour	44-55
raisin	40-50
rye	
American	43-54
pumpernickel	43-54
salt-rising	42-53
white, enriched, made with 1%-2% nonfat dry milk	43-54
whole-wheat, made with 2% nonfat dry milk	45-56
water	43-54
breadcrumbs, dry, grated	55-69
broccoli	
frozen, chopped	20-25
raw, partially trimmed	18-23
brussels sprouts, raw, good quality	19-24
buckwheat flour, dark	41-51
butter	11-14
butterfish, northern, raw	32-40
buttermilk, fluid, cultured	14-18
butternuts	
in shell	11-14
shelled	74-93

cabbage, common varieties
- dehydrated — 59-74
- raw, head trimmed — 18-23

cakes made from home-type recipe
- angelfood — 36-45
- Boston cream pie — 35-44
- most — 36-45

cake mix
- angelfood — 39-49
- most — 31-39

candy
- caramels, plain or chocolate — 32-40
- chocolate, milk
  - plain — 44-55
  - with almonds — 48-60
  - with peanuts — 58-73
- chocolate, sweet — 40-50
- chocolate-coated
  - peanuts — 62-78
  - raisins — 36-45
- hard — 26-33
- jelly beans — 25-31
- marshmallows — 25-31
- peanut bars — 63-79
- peanut brittle — 38-48

carp, raw, whole — 23-29

carrots
- canned, regular pack — 21-26
- raw, without tops — 19-24

cashew nuts — 61-76

catfish, freshwater, fillets, raw — 66-83

cauliflower, raw, fully trimmed — 18-23

celery, all varieties — 14-18

chard, swiss, raw, good quality — 16-20

cheeses
- natural cheeses
  - blue or roquefort type — 83-104
  - brick — 85-106
  - camembert (domestic) — 70-88
  - cheddar (American) — 99-124
  - cottage cheese, creamed — 54-68
  - cottage cheese, un-creamed — 63-79
  - cream — 39-49
  - limburger — 82-103
  - parmesan — 136-170
  - Swiss (domestic) — 102-128
- pasteurized process
  - American — 94-118
  - cheese food (American) — 85-106
  - cheese spread (American) — 68-85
  - pimento (American) — 94-118
  - Swiss — 100-125

cherries
- canned, red, heavy sirup
  - sour, without pits — 20-25
  - sweet — 20-25
- frozen, sour, red, un-sweetened — 19-24
- raw, sweet — 14-18

chicken, raw
- fryers, ready-to-cook — 49-61

Food	Range
cut-up parts	
back	38-48
breast	61-76
drumstick	44-55
neck	33-41
thigh	53-66
wing	38-48
roasters, ready-to-cook	54-68
hens and cocks, ready-to-cook	54-68
chicken, canned, meat only, boned	90-113
chicken potpie, frozen	41-51
chickpeas or **garbanzos,** mature seeds, dry, raw	51-65
chickory, witloof, raw	8-10
chili con carne, canned	
with beans	38-48
without beans	50-63
chocolate, bitter or baking	58-73

Food	Range
chocolate sirup	
fudge type	31-39
thin type	28-35
chop suey with meat, canned	16-20
chow mein with chicken, canned	13-16
clams, raw, hard or round, meat and liquid in shell	15-19
cocoa and chocolate flavored beverage powders	
with nonfat dry milk	53-66
without milk	33-41
mix for hot chocolate	42-53
cod	
dried, salted	107-134
raw, flesh only	67-84
collards, leaves without stems, raw	22-28
cookies	
assorted, packaged	44-55

Food	Range
fig bars	42-53
oatmeal with raisins	49-61
peanut	56-70
raisin	41-51
sandwich type	44-55
sugar wafers	44-55
vanilla wafers	44-55
cookie mix, plain, enriched	38-48
corn	
field, whole-grain, raw	37-46
sweet	
canned	
cream style	20-25
vacuum pack, yellow	21-26
wet pack, white and yellow	19-24
frozen, kernels cut off cob	20-25
raw, on cob	11-14
corn flour	31-39
corn grits, degermed, enriched	38-48

corn products used mainly as ready-to-eat breakfast cereals
corn flakes — 45-56
  added nutrients — 40-50
  added nutrients, sugar covered — 46-58
corn, puffed
  added nutrients — 39-49
  presweetened
    added nutrients — 43-54
    cocoa-flavored — 42-53
    fruit-flavored
corn, shredded, added nutrients — 44-55
corn, rice, wheat flakes, mixed — 44-55

cornbread mix — 40-50

cornmeal, white or yellow
  bolted (nearly whole-grain) — 36-45
  whole ground — 36-45

cornstarch — 19-24

cowpeas, including blackeye peas
  immature seeds, raw, shelled — 24-30
  mature, dry — 57-71

crab
  canned — 72-90
  cooked, meat only — 67-84

crackers
  animal — 45-56
  cheese — 52-65
  graham, plain — 44-55
  saltines — 47-59
  sandwich type, peanut-cheese — 59-74
  soda — 47-59
  whole wheat — 47-59

cranberries
  canned sauce, sweetened — 13-16
  cocktail juice, bottled — 6-8
  raw — 7-9

crappie, white, raw, flesh only — 62-78

FOODS AND THEIR FAIR VALUE RANGES

cream, fluid
  half-and-half — 19-24
  heavy, whipping — 15-19
  light, coffee or table — 18-23
  light, whipping — 16-20

cream substitutes, dried, containing:
  cream, skim milk, lactose — 58-73
  cream, skim milk, lactose, sodium hexametaphosphate — 74-93

cucumbers, raw, whole — 12-15

currants, raw
  black, European — 18-23
  red and white — 16-20

dandelion greens, raw, trimmed — 25-31

dates
  with pits — 27-34
  without pits — 30-38

doughnuts	
cake type	45-56
yeast-leavened	48-60
duck, domesticated, ready-to-cook	51-64
Eggbeater (frozen)	62-78
Eggright (dry)	205-256
lemon juice	
dried, whole	177-221
raw, whole, fresh	48-60
eggplant, raw	12-15
endive, raw, good quality	13-16
farina, enriched	
instant cooking	41-51
regular cooking	40-50
fats, cooking (vegetable)	45-56
figs	
canned, extra heavy sirup	17-21
dried	33-58
raw	12-15
filberts, shelled	60-75
finnan haddie (smoked haddock), flesh only, raw	76-95
flatfishes (flounders, soles and sanddabs), raw	
flesh only	62-78
whole	23-29
fruit cocktail, canned	
heavy sirup	16-20
water pack	14-18
gelatin desserts, plain	13-16
grapefuit	
juice, canned	
sweetened	14-18
unsweetened	13-16
raw, all varieties	10-13
grapefruit and orange juice, blended	
canned	
sweetened	13-16
unsweetened	13-16
frozen concentrate, unsweetened	24-30
grapes, raw	10-13
grape juice	
canned or bottled	10-13
frozen concentrate, sweetened	21-26
haddock	
raw	
flesh only	67-84
whole	33-41
smoked	83-104
halibut, raw, Atlantic & Pacific	
flesh only	76-95
whole	45-56
halibut, smoked	77-96

FOODS AND THEIR FAIR VALUE RANGES

Food	Range
heart, beef, lean, raw	62-78
herring	
Atlantic, raw	
flesh only	69-86
whole	36-45
canned	
in tomato sauce	64-80
plain	78-98
Pacific, flesh only, raw	65-81
pickled, Bismarck type	77-96
salted or brined	69-86
smoked	
bloaters	71-89
kippered	80-100
honey, strained or extracted	23-29
horseradish, prepared	16-20
ice cream and frozen custard	
regular	
approximately 10% fat	27-34
approximately 12% fat	26-33
rich, approximately 16% fat	21-26
ice milk	26-33

Food	Range
ices, water, lime	8-10
jams and preserves	34-43
jellies	30-38
Jerusalem artichokes, raw	12-15
kale	
leaves without stems, raw	23-29
frozen	22-28
kidneys, beef, raw	58-73
kohlrabi, stems only, raw	13-16
lake trout, raw	
drawn	28-35
fillets	71-89
lamb, choice cut	
leg	
with bone	57-71
without bone	67-84
loin	
with bone	55-69
without bone	62-78

Food	Range
rib	
with bone	48-60
without bone	58-73
lard	5-6
lemons with peel, raw	12-15
lemon juice	
canned or bottled, unsweetened	15-19
frozen	
single-strength	15-19
concentrate	28-35
lemonade concentrate, frozen	21-26
lentils, mature seeds, dry, raw, whole	58-73
lettuce, crisphead varieties, good quality raw	9-11
liver, raw	
beef	79-99
calf	77-96
chicken, all classes	78-98

hog	80-100
lamb	82-103
turkey, all classes	81-101
lobster, northern, raw	
meat only	57-71
whole	15-19
macaroni	
enriched	46-58
unenriched	41-51
macaroni and cheese, canned	16-20
mackerel	
Atlantic	
canned	80-100
whole, raw	41-51
Pacific	
canned	80-100
dressed	60-75
flesh only	82-103
mangos, raw	13-16
margarine	47-59
marmalade, citrus	26-33

milk, cow	
fluid (pasteurized and raw)	
whole, 3.5% fat	14-18
skim	14-18
canned	
condensed (sweetened)	36-45
evaporated (unsweetened)	25-31
dry	
skim	
instant	77-96
regular	77-96
whole	73-91
malted	
beverage	17-21
dry powder	52-65
chocolate drink, fluid, commercial	
made with skim milk	14-18
made with whole milk	14-18
millet, whole grain	37-46
molasses, cane	
first extraction, or light	19-24
second extraction, or medium	18-23

third extraction, or black-strap	16-20
muffin mix, with enriched flour	37-46
muffins, baked from home-type recipe	
corn, made with enriched cornmeal	41-51
plain, made with enriched flour	41-51
mushrooms, raw, good quality	19-24
muskmelons, raw	
cantaloupes	11-14
casaba	9-11
honeydew	9-11
mussels, Atlantic and Pacific, raw meat and liquid in shell	19-24
mustard greens, raw	19-24
nectarines, raw	14-18
noodles, chow mein, canned	49-61

169

FOODS AND THEIR FAIR VALUE RANGES

Food	Range
noodles, egg, enriched	47-59
oat products used mainly as hot breakfast cereals	
oat cereal with wheat germ and soy grits	54-68
oat flakes, instant cooking	44-55
oat granules, quick-cooking	45-56
oat and wheat cereal	46-58
oatmeal (rolled oats)	44-55
oat products used mainly as ready-to-eat breakfast cereals	
flaked	57-71
puffed	51-64
puffed, sugar coated	44-55
shredded	67-84
oils, salad or cooking	45-56
okra	
frozen, cuts and pods	16-20
raw, good quality	15-19
olives, pickled, canned, or bottled	
green	
with pits	13-16
without pits	13-16
ripe (ascolano)	
with pits	12-15
without pits	12-15
ripe, salt cured, oil-coated	25-31
onions	
mature, dry	
dehydrated, flaked	62-78
raw	17-21
young, green, raw	14-18
Welsh, raw	16-20
orange juice	
canned	
sweetened	15-19
unsweetened	15-19
unsweetened concentrate	35-44
dehydrated	53-66
frozen, concentrate, unsweetened	29-36
oranges, raw	
used for fruit	14-18
used for juice	14-18
orange and apricot juice drink, canned	13-16
oyster stew, frozen, condensed	26-33
oysters, eastern, raw	
in shell	4-5
meat only	35-44
pancake and waffle mixes	
buckwheat and other cereal flours	40-50
plain and buttermilk with enriched flour	38-48
parsnips, raw	14-18
pastinas, enriched, egg	46-58
pate de foie gras, canned	52-65
peach nectar, canned	10-13
peaches	
canned	
heavy sirup	19-24

Food	Value range
peaches (cont.)	
juice pack	17-21
dehydrated	42-53
dried, sulfured	35-44
frozen, sliced, sweetened	17-21
raw, peeled fruit	12-15
peanut butter made with:	
small amount of added fat and salt	79-99
small amount of added fat, sweetener, and salt	76-95
moderate amount of added fat, sweetener, and salt	75-94
peanut spread	68-85
peanuts, roasted	
in shell	55-69
shelled	81-101
pear nectar, canned	9-11
pears	
canned	
heavy sirup	15-19
juice pack	14-18
water pack	13-16
dried, sulfured	31-39
raw for fruit	10-13
peas, green, immature	
canned, regular pack	
Alaska (early or June)	19-24
sweet	19-24
frozen	24-30
raw	
in pod	10-13
shelled	26-33
peas, dry, mature seeds, raw	
split, without seed coat	66-83
whole	66-83
peas and carrots, frozen	26-33
pecans	
in shell	28-35
shelled	55-69
peppers, hot, chili	
immature, green	
canned	
chili sauce	25-31
pods, excluding seeds	26-33
raw	21-26
mature, red	
canned, chili sauce	31-39
dried	
chili powder	83-104
pods	85-106
raw	
pods, excluding seeds	30-38
pods, including seeds	40-50
peppers, sweet garden variety	
green, raw	22-28
red, raw	28-35
perch, raw	
yellow	
flesh only	71-89
whole	30-38
white	
flesh only	72-90
whole	28-35

FOODS AND THEIR FAIR VALUE RANGES

Food	Range
persimmons, raw	
Japanese or kaki varieties	
with seeds	14-18
without seeds	15-19
native	17-21
pickles	
cucumber	
dill	11-14
fresh (as bread-and-butter pickles)	14-18
sour	10-13
sweet	18-23
chowchow	
sour	15-19
sweet	19-24
relish	
sour	13-16
sweet	19-24
pies	
baked, piecrust made with enriched flour	
apple	30-38
cherry	30-38
chocolate chiffon	39-49
custard	31-39
lemon chiffon	37-46
lemon meringue	29-36
mince	30-38
peach	32-40
pecan	40-50
pineapple	29-36
pineapple chiffon	37-46
pumpkin	34-43
strawberry	31-39
frozen in unbaked form	
apple	21-26
cherry	31-39
coconut custard	30-38
piecrust mix, including stick form	42-53
pimentos, canned	21-26
pineapple	
canned	
heavy sirup	20-25
juice pack	19-24
water pack	16-20
raw	10-13
pineapple juice	
canned, unsweetened	12-15
frozen concentrate, unsweetened	21-26
pineapple and grapefruit juice drink, canned	11-14
pizza, with cheese	
from home-type recipe, baked	
with cheese topping	43-54
with sausage topping	37-46
frozen, partially baked	33-41
plate dinners, frozen, commercial	
beef pot roast, whole oven-browned potatoes, peas, and corn	60-75
chicken, fried; mashed potatoes, mixed vegetables	60-75
meat loaf with tomato sauce, mashed potatoes, and peas	46-58
turkey, sliced; mashed potatoes, and peas	46-58

plums
canned	
greengage	14-18
purple (Italian prunes)	
heavy sirup	17-21
water pack	15-19
raw	
damson	11-14
prune-type	12-15

pollock, raw
drawn	35-44
fillets	74-93

pompano, raw
flesh only	73-91
whole	41-51

popcorn, unpopped — 38-48

pork, fresh, medium-fat, raw
bacon or belly, without skin	34-43
Boston butt	
with bone and skin	55-69
without bone and skin	58-73
ham	
with bone and skin	52-65
without bone and skin	60-75
loin	
with bone	52-65
without bone	64-80
picnic	
with bone and skin	50-63
without bone and skin	59-74
shoulder	
without bone and skin	49-61
spareribs	
with bone	36-45
without bone	55-69

pork, cured, canned ham — 74-93

pork, long-cure, dry, ham, medium-fat
with bone and skin	60-75
without bone and skin	67-84

pork and gravy, canned (90% pork, 10% gravy) — 68-85

potato chips — 52-65

FOODS AND THEIR FAIR VALUE RANGES

potato flour — 34-43

potatoes
canned, solids and liquid	15-19
dehydrated, mashed	
flakes without milk	44-55
granules with milk	49-61
granules without milk	45-56
frozen	
french fried	27-34
mashed	18-23
raw	14-18

pretzels — 44-55

prune juice, canned or bottled — 12-15

prunes, dried, large — 30-38

pudding mix with starch base, chocolate, regular — 28-35

pumpkin
canned	21-26
raw	13-16

radishes, raw, without tops — 10-13

FOODS AND THEIR FAIR VALUE RANGES

Food	Range
raisins, natural	35-44
raspberries, red	
canned	16-20
frozen, sweetened	17-21
raw	13-16
rhubarb	
frozen, sweetened	13-16
raw, without leaves	9-11
rice	
brown, raw	34-43
white	
common varieties, enriched, raw	32-40
long-grain, parboiled	33-41
rice products used mainly as hot breakfast cereals	
rice, granulated, added nutrients	33-41
rice products used mainly as ready-to-eat breakfast cereals, with added nutrients	
rice flakes	43-54
rice, puffed or oven-popped, presweetened	
honey	41-51
honey or cocoa plus fat	42-53
rice, shredded	42-53
rice with protein concentrate, mainly:	
casein	96-120
wheat gluten	66-83
rolls and buns	
ready-to-serve	
Danish pastry	44-55
hard, enriched flour	45-56
plain, enriched flour	42-53
sweet	40-50
whole wheat	43-54
partially baked (brown and serve), enriched flour	36-45
roll dough, frozen, enriched flour	32-40
rutabagas, without tops	13-16
rye	
flours	
dark	47-59
light	33-41
medium	40-50
whole grain	39-49
rye wafers, whole grain	50-63
salad dressings, commercial	
blue and roquefort cheese, regular	46-58
French, regular	28-35
Italian, regular	34-43
mayonnaise	45-56
Russian	35-44
thousand island, regular	34-43
salmon	
Atlantic	
canned, solids and liquid	80-100
raw	
flesh only	85-106
whole	56-70
smoked	77-96
sockeye (red), canned	80-100
sandwich spread with chopped pickle, regular	30-38

FOODS AND THEIR FAIR VALUE RANGES

Food	Value
sardines	
Atlantic, canned in oil	85-106
Pacific, canned	
in brine or mustard	71-89
in tomato sauce	74-93
sauerkraut, canned	16-20
sausage, cold cuts, and lun-	
cheon meats	
bologna	
all samples	49-61
all meat	53-66
country-style sausage	55-69
deviled ham, canned	56-70
frankfurters	
all samples, raw	47-59
canned	55-69
liverwurst	
fresh	62-78
smoked	59-74
luncheon meat	
boiled ham	75-94
pork, cured ham or	
shoulder, spiced, or un-	
spiced, canned	62-78
meat loaf	65-81
meat, potted (includes beef,	
chicken, and turkey)	68-85
salami, dry	88-110
scrapple	39-49
Vienna sausage, canned	58-73
scallops, bay and sea, raw	54-68
shad or American shad	
canned	64-80
raw, flesh only	72-90
sherbet, orange	10-13
shrimp	
canned, solids and liquid	
raw	60-75
in shell	46-58
flesh only	67-84
sirup	
cane	20-25
maple	20-25
sorghum	20-25
table blends	
chiefly corn	22-28
chiefly cane and maple	20-25
smelt, Atlantic, raw, whole	38-48
soups, commerical	
canned	
asparagus, cream of	16-20
bean with pork	33-41
beef broth	21-26
beef noodle	19-24
celery, cream of	16-20
chicken consomme	16-20
chicken, cream of	18-23
chicken gumbo	17-21
chicken noodle	18-23
chicken with rice	17-21
chicken vegetable	22-28
clam chowder, manhattan	17-21
minestrone	25-31
mushroom, cream of	23-29
onion	28-35
pea, green	26-33
pea, split	34-43
tomato	18-23
turkey noodle	21-26
vegetable beef	26-33
vegetable with beef broth	17-21

FOODS AND THEIR FAIR VALUE RANGES

Food	Range
vegetarian vegetable	20-25
dehydrated mix	
beef noodle	71-89
chicken noodle	73-91
chicken rice	53-66
onion	73-91
pea, green	97-121
frozen	
vegetable with beef	30-38
soybean flour	
full-fat	80-100
high-fat	84-105
low-fat	85-106
soybean protein	125-156
spaghetti, enriched	104-130
spaghetti in tomato sauce with cheese, canned	29-36
spaghetti with meat balls in tomato sauce, canned	28-35
spinach	
canned, regular pack	20-25
frozen, chopped	21-26
raw, good quality	
trimmed	21-26
untrimmed	18-23
squash	
frozen	
summer	11-14
winter	14-18
raw, good quality	
summer	11-14
winter	14-18
strawberries	
frozen, sliced, sweetened	21-26
raw, good quality	13-16
sturgeon, smoked	44-55
succotash, frozen	15-19
sugars	
beet or cane	
brown	26-33
granulated	27-34
powdered	27-34
maple	25-31
sweet potatoes	
canned, regular pack in sirup	23-29
raw	22-28
tangerines, raw	13-16
tapioca, dry	23-29
tartar sauce, regular	35-44
tomatoes	
canned, regular pack	22-28
raw, ripe, whole	18-23
tomato catsup, bottled	23-29
tomato chili sauce, bottled	23-29
tomato juice, canned or bottled	
concentrate	24-30
regular pack	11-14
tomato juice cocktail, canned or bottled	11-14

Food	Range
tomato paste, canned	35-44
tomato puree, canned, regular	18-23
trout, rainbow, raw, flesh only	82-103
tuna, canned	
in oil	97-121
in water	100-125
turkey	
canned, meat only	81-101
potpie, frozen	36-45
raw, ready-to-cook	55-69
turnips, raw, without tops	11-14
turnip greens	
frozen	21-26
raw, trimmed	21-26
veal, medium-fat	
flank	
with bone	62-78
without bone	63-79
loin	
with bone	60-75
without bone	71-89
rib	
with bone	56-70
without bone	70-88
vegetable juice cocktail, canned	9-11
vegetables, mixed, frozen	20-25
waffles, frozen, enriched flour	31-39
waffle mix, enriched flour	40-50
walnuts	
black, shelled	75-94
Persian or English	
in shell	30-38
shelled	70-88
watermelon, raw	8-10
wheat bran, crude	51-64
wheat flours	
patent	38-48
all-purpose, enriched	
bread flour, enriched	40-50
cake, or pastry flour	29-36
whole	42-53
wheat germ, crude	62-78
wheat products used mainly as hot breakfast cereals	
wheat, rolled	40-50
wheat, whole meal	45-56
wheat and malted barley, toasted	
instant-cooking	42-53
quick-cooking	39-49
wheat products used mainly as ready-to-eat cereals	
wheat flakes	50-63
wheat germ, toasted	80-100
wheat, puffed	57-71
wheat, puffed, with honey	45-56
wheat, shredded	49-61
wheat, shredded, with malt	49-61
wheat and malted barley flakes	48-60
wheat and malted barley granules	50-63

yam, tuber, raw   15-19

yoghurt
   made with skim milk   15-19
   made with whole milk   14-18

Zwieback   50-63